6.00

WATERFOWL
STUDIES

WATERFOWL STUDIES

BRUCE BURK

Winchester Press

All photographs and drawings by the author.

Waterfowl classified after Delacour, *Waterfowl of the World,* Dover.

Library of Congress Catalog Card Number: 76-17920
ISBN: 87691-180-7

Library of Congress Cataloging in Publication Data
Burk, Bruce.
    Waterfowl studies.
    Bibliography: p.
    1. Waterfowl—Pictorial works.   2. Birds—North
America—Pictorial works.   3. Zoological illustration—
Pictorial works. I. Title.
QL696.A5B8   598.2'924'0222   76-17920
ISBN 0-87691-180-7

Winchester Press
1421 South Sheridan
Tulsa, Oklahoma 74114

Printed in the United States of America
6 7 8 9 — 83 82 81

ACKNOWLEDGMENTS

I am deeply indebted to my many carver-artist friends who encouraged me to proceed with this undertaking. I hope the results will repay them in a small way for their contributions.

My most sincere thanks to the following friends who assisted me in obtaining the photographs and material contained in this book: Bill Bartha, Rosamond, California; Jerry Berman, San Bernardino, California; John Cowan, Gridley, California; Bryan Davies, Ladner, British Columbia; Dave and Gladys Hagerbaumer, Independence, Oregon; Dr. Paul A. Johnsgard, Lincoln, Nebraska; Gene Mellon, Sherman Oaks, California; Jim Northern, Los Angeles County Museum; Mr. and Mrs. Charles Pilling, Seattle, Washington; Bob and Joyce Reed, Independence, Oregon; Mike Shlaudeman, Altadena, California; Dr. Ken Stager, Los Angeles County Museum; Bill and Barbara Toth, Pebble Beach, California; and Dick Trethewey, Mapleridge, British Columbia.

The original black and white prints for this book were made by Frank Schultz, Saugus, California. I would like to express my gratitude for his excellent work and fine cooperation.

CONTENTS

INTRODUCTION

Although this collection of waterfowl photos has been assembled primarily to aid the artist in making realistic bird carvings and paintings, these pictures will also be of interest to other bird lovers and naturalists. Many superb bird photographs have been published in recent years, but most publications seldom present more than one photo of a particular species. Here, for the first time, the more popular waterfowl of this continent are pictured in a variety of poses taken at different angles—all aimed at helping the artist to duplicate accurately body form, position, and plumage detail.

The life histories and personal traits of the various waterfowl species have been thoroughly covered by many noted ornithologists (some of their publications are listed in the Appendix). Since there is little I can add to their skilled observations, the text in this book has been kept to a minimum to provide maximum space for photographs.

The popularity of wildfowl paintings and bird carvings is growing rapidly. This increased interest people have in realistic wildlife art in general, and wildfowl art in particular, can be attributed to a number of factors—the desire to return to realism in art; the recent awareness of nature brought about by the urgent need for conservation of natural resources; increasing difficulty in being able to find and enjoy wildlife in unspoiled habitats; more leisure time for bird watching, hunting, and related activities; the widespread interest in collecting old decoys; and the soundness of wildlife art as an investment.

Probably the most important reason for this increased popularity is the great improvement in the quality of wildlife art during the past decade or two. Some of this improvement can be attributed to better techniques, but the availability of good wildlife photographs has played by far the most important role in the development of wildlife art. The artist of not too many years ago had to rely completely on his eye and memory when he attempted to reproduce natural form, movement, color, and detail. Many movements of wildfowl are much too rapid to be discerned by the naked eye, and their structural detail is so complex that only a camera can capture and record these most important positions and features.

The late Richard Bishop devoted most of his life to realistic wildfowl art. He was one of the very first artists to become dissatisfied with using the standard, and usually inaccurate, positions and poses of birds. By firsthand observation and the use of an early Bell and Howell slow-motion movie camera, Bishop eventually worked out over 1,000 accurate sketches of wildfowl in their many positions on the ground and in the air. The great popularity of his paintings and etchings over many years is his reward for these efforts, and he must be ranked as one of the most outstanding wildfowl artists of all times. Bishop was responsible for Edgar M. Queeny's interest in wildfowl photography and many of his fine sketches are shown in Queeny's classic *Prairie Wings*. Today, an increasing number of successful artists take many of their own reference photographs, not only of birds and animals, but of natural habitats and backgrounds.

While young compared to most arts, wildlife photography is older than most people realize. George Shiras III, the father of wildlife photography, was producing excellent black and white photographs of a variety of birds and animals as early as 1890. The first of his many contributions to the *National Geographic* magazine was published in 1905. These fine articles, beautifully illustrated by his magnificent photographs, were eventually printed in book form, *Hunting Wildlife with Camera and Flashlight* (Volumes I and II). Compared to the many excellent cameras, lenses, and films available today, his equipment was incredibly crude, unwieldy, and slow — his results are a great tribute to his outstanding ingenuity and patience. In addition to his reputation as a wildlife photographer, Shiras became one of the most widely known field naturalists in America, and he devoted a large portion of his life to the conservation of birds, animals, and habitats. The famed Migratory Bird Treaty Bill was introduced by him during his term in Congress (1903–1905).

For those interested in wildlife photography, most of my early bird pictures were taken with 400mm and 640mm Novoflex Nesting Tele lenses and 35mm Topcon Super D camera bodies. Practically all of the later photographs were made with a 500mm Auto-Topcor lens. A tripod was used occasionally, but the majority of the pictures were taken with only a gunstock-type mount for support. Kodak Tri X black and white film, boosted a few times as high as ASA 1600, was used. Color work was done with Kodak High Speed Ektachrome boosted to ASA 400 so that higher shutter speeds and smaller apertures could be utilized.

The artist should be aware that some of the photographs in this book—also in many other publications—are of captive birds. Most captive birds have been "pinioned"—the outermost ten feathers (the primaries) of one wing have been removed to prevent flight. The long primary feathers of each wing on waterfowl when folded lie neatly against the flanks and usually cross, or at least meet, above the rump or tail. If the photograph shows the unpinioned side of the bird, the pictured primaries, secondaries, tertials, and scapulars almost always appear in a fairly normal manner, the only difference being that the tips of the primary group on the other wing, which would normally show, are nonexistent. In some cases, the profile of the upper rear part of the bird is altered to a degree because the single group of primaries and the feathers under which they lie are not as well supported as when there are two groups of primaries crossed over each other. Also, some pinioned birds, because of their sedentary lives, may not be as trim as active flying birds. By carefully studying both pinioned and unpinioned birds, as well as photographs, the artist can soon make the necessary allowances caused by the removal of one set of primaries.

Most male ducks experience plumage changes. All birds replace their worn feathers periodically by molting—a process that normally goes by unnoticed except in the case of male ducks. About the time the female settles down to the incubation routine, most male ducks leave their mates and band together. At that time, the bright, breeding plumage of the drake is replaced by a special, or "eclipse" plumage which, in most cases, is quite similar to the females. Shortly after this molt is completed, a second molt starts and the female-type plumage is very gradually replaced over a period of several months by the more colorful breeding plumage.

It was formerly believed that this eclipse molt was limited only to male ducks of the Northern Hemisphere; however, it is now known that at least the cinnamon teal of South America, the Australian and New Zealand shovelers, and some Australian teal have similar molts. There are variations in the eclipse molt with the different duck species. Some of these differences will be noted in the chapter for the particular species.

Practically all paintings and carvings depict the male duck in his breeding plumage. Therefore, unless otherwise noted, male ducks shown in this book are in this plumage. Many ducks taken during the normal hunting season have not yet acquired their full breeding plumage. Familiarity with the eclipse molt is obviously important when the artist uses duck specimens for feather pattern and color. The excellent color plates painted by T. M. Shortt in Francis H. Kortright's *The Ducks, Geese, and Swans of North America* and by Peter Scott in Jean Delacour's four-volume masterpiece, *The Waterfowl of the World* portray the different male ducks in their eclipse plumage.

PROLOGUE

Although there are many birds equally at home on water, the term "waterfowl" commonly refers to members of the Anatidae family which includes ducks, geese, and swans. Great diversities in size, shape, color, habitat requirements, and behavior exist between the individual species; however, a few common features characterize this family. All have well-insulated, buoyant bodies; all have powerful legs; all have feet adapted for swimming with three forward-pointing toes joined by webs, and a small, undeveloped hind toe; all have downy young capable of swimming shortly after hatching; and all have bills edged with toothlike serrations, called *lamellae*, on both the upper and lower mandibles. The family Anatidae is a fairly large one, with members distributed over most of the world, though the majority of the waterfowl population is found in the North Temperate Zone. We, in the continental United States, are fortunate to have approximately forty-five species as inhabitants for at least a part of the year and several more as occasional visitors.

Certain structural modifications have enabled the various waterfowl to adapt to a wide variety of environments. Most important of these modifications are those that permit them to take advantage of the different available food sources.

All species are proficient swimmers and most, if not all, can dive, although some do only to escape danger —usually when they are incapable of flight. Compared to the dabblers, diving ducks have legs located farther to the rear, spaced farther apart laterally, and have much larger feet — features that enable them to dive expertly and allow some species to obtain food at times from incredible depths approaching 180 feet. However, their normal diving depth is probably less than 15 feet. Their usual submergence time is 90 seconds or less, depending on the availability of food. Although there does not appear to be any recorded data, the time required to dive to the greater depths, gather food, and rise to the surface would obviously be considerably longer. It is known, however, that ducks can withstand involuntary submergence for durations up to 16 minutes. Some divers — the mergansers and buffleheads — swim with such speed underwater they are able to catch fish. During the breeding season, the harlequin duck becomes adapted to life in the wildest of rushing

An expert diver in action—American merganser.

mountain streams and can actually swim near or at the bottom against these swift currents while collecting food.

The same features that enable these birds to dive so efficiently — leg location and foot size — restrict their movement on land and, as a result, they are seen only infrequently out of the water. Actually, all of the diving ducks can walk moderately well if necessary, and even run, except the little ruddy who is almost helpless on land. There is little need for the divers to inhabit land as all of their living requirements, except nesting sites, are adequately provided by the water and the animal and vegetable life found therein. A few of the waterfowl species — the eiders, the scoters, and the brant — spend almost all of their time during the winter in salt water and, by means of well-developed glands (located above the eyes) that excrete the salt from ocean water, are able to subsist without fresh water.

At the other extreme, the Hawaiian goose (or nene) seldom goes into water even when it is available. As a result, his feet now have small webs and are poorly adapted for swimming.

Dabbling ducks are excellent surface swimmers and, if the necessity arises, most can dive fairly well. They have become adapted to life in small, shallow bodies of fresh water where food can be easily obtained without completely submerging. Also, during some times of the year, much of their food is found on land. Their bodies, therefore, have become modified to meet these specific conditions — modifications that permit them to walk much better than diving ducks and make them generally more at home on land. Geese, except for the brant and emperor, acquire most of their food on land and return to water mainly to drink and for protection. Their smaller feet and longer legs, located farther forward and closer together, permit them to walk and run easily without the characteristic waddle of ducks. Swans, with short legs and very large feet, walk with more effort. Most of their food consists of aquatic plants and a great deal of their time is spent on the water.

There are many variations in bill size and shape among the different waterfowl species. Nature has wonderfully provided these modifications, along with other capabilities, so that waterfowl can exist on the variety of foods, both vegetable and animal, found in their different habitats.

The bills of the dabbling ducks are quite similar and are adapted for tearing loose and eating vegetable matter and some animal matter. In addition, their bills are especially adapted for straining small organisms from mud and water. Shovelers, cinnamon teal, and blue-winged teal — in that order — have the greatest development of strainers (*lamellae*) for obtaining food in this manner. The diving ducks have larger differences in bill size and shape. Bills of the pochards and the goldeneyes are very similar to dabbling ducks, while scoters and eiders have heavier bills capable of crushing small mollusks. Mergansers have the most highly specialized bill of the waterfowl. It is cylindrical and slender in shape and especially adapted for seizing and holding live, slippery fish. The bills of geese are

Mallard pair feed in shallow water by "up-ending."

Highly specialized bills (mounted birds).

Northern shoveler, male.

American merganser, female.

adapted for clipping vegetable matter, usually grasses, close to the ground. Swans have large bills, intermediate in shape between ducks and geese, that are adapted for tearing loose and eating aquatic plants.

As flyers, waterfowl are marvelous! They excel almost all other birds when speed, range, endurance, and maximum flight altitudes are compared. The published flight speed records of waterfowl (and other birds) contain many inconsistencies. There appears to be considerable confusion in regard to air speed (the speed the bird is flying relative to the surrounding air) and ground speed (the speed the bird is flying relative to the ground). One ornithologist reported speeds of 72 mph for the canvasback, popularly considered the fastest of waterfowl. Another ornithologist questioned this speed, and records of mallards attaining speeds of 70 mph, but reported that eiders, whose normal flight speed is 50 mph, were able to fly at 15–20 mph into a wind of 80–90 mph. This would be the equivalent to actual flight speeds of 95–110 mph in still air! Except for those flight records established by means of aircraft, most do not take into account wind velocity; therefore, records of this type reflect ground speeds that, except for conditions of no wind, are meaningless. Other unknowns such as the degree of exertion and whether or not the bird is in level flight are ignored. Birds, like aircraft, have a maximum level flight speed, a cruising speed range, and a stalling speed. They fly at maximum effort only for short distances, usually to escape danger. It has been reported that waterfowl fly slower on local flights than when on migration flights. If based on ground speed, it may be true, as birds are known to take advantage of favorable winds when migrating. Generally, and perhaps more realistically, most waterfowl cruise at air speeds between 20 and 40 mph and, under certain conditions, may be able to attain speeds of 40–60 mph.

The range and endurance of some waterfowl, especially the blue-winged and cinnamon teals and pintails, have been accurately established many times by the recovery of banded birds. Records of these remarkable flyers averaging over 100 miles per day on long migratory flights in excess of 2,000 miles are not uncommon.

Although waterfowl normally fly at considerably lower altitudes, geese and swans sometimes migrate at altitudes as high as 10,000 feet. Snow geese have been reported at estimated altitudes in excess of 25,000 feet. Waterfowl inhabit lakes in the Andes at elevations of 13,000 feet, and obviously are capable of taking off in this low-density air — a feat requiring tremendous power.

Waterfowl, most diving ducks excepted, possess great flight maneuverability. To quote Queeny, "One eminent ornithologist has written that ducks are incapable of vertical flight; another that humming birds are the only birds able to fly backwards. Here is the beginning, at least, of vertical flight [referring to a photograph of a female mallard rising vertically from the water]. I have a slow-motion picture of a mallard rising vertically to the top of a hundred-foot tree. Then it flew backward some distance, turned itself around, and continued on in normal flight."

Nature has provided additional flight maneuverability to two duck species who inhabit heavily wooded areas — the Carolina wood duck and the hooded merganser. These ducks have much larger tails, which enable them to fly at high speed, twisting and dodging through the trees.

The wings of waterfowl have also been modified to meet their individual needs. Dabbling ducks inhabit small bodies of water, often just puddles, usually heavily overgrown with tules. Their safety and continued use of these habitats depend on their ability to take off vertically and quickly from very tight quarters. Nature has provided them with considerably larger wings, relative to their body weight, to meet this requirement. Diving ducks are generally found on large, open bodies of water. Large wings would hinder their diving capabilities; therefore, nature gave them smaller wings — ones that were quite adequate for efficient flight provided that some forward speed was obtained by pattering over the surface of the water for a short distance during take off.

Many birds migrate, but few make their migrations as manifest and spectacular as waterfowl. Millions of people, young and old alike, are thrilled each spring by the long, converging lines of geese and the hordes of ducks tirelessly winging their way northward unerringly to their own favorite nesting grounds, often to the exact nesting site of the previous year. Even at night their migration is made evident by the unforgettable, deep, resonant *ah-honk* of the Canadas and the yelping of the snow geese. For many, after the cold and seemingly endless winter, they bring the promise of warm weather and green foliage; for others, they arouse a latent yearning to be free of earthly bounds and to wing north with them.

While the migration of waterfowl is spectacular and beautiful to man who is privileged to see only a fleeting glimpse of one small segment, it is a serious business to the remarkably intelligent and unbelievably persevering creatures who make these incredible flights, often as far as 3,000 miles. Prior to starting, they must be in perfect physical condition and have acquired during the wintering period reserve energy in the form of body fat. They must plan their start and schedule their flights so that they will arrive at the nesting grounds at the proper time, an accomplishment requiring superb navigation, often under adverse weather conditions and at night — all done without benefit of maps, electronic navigational aids, and modern meteorological information. If they arrive at their destination too soon — before most of the snow has melted — they will be faced with a wait during which time there will be little food. If they arrive too late, there will be insufficient time to incubate the eggs and rear the young to the point where they are capable of making the long, southward flight before the fall freeze-up. The female must arrive on the nesting grounds with enough physical stamina to withstand the rigors of producing eggs and incubating them — a period when she has little time to forage for food and may lose one-fourth of her body weight. After the eggs are hatched, the parents, in addition to rearing their young and molting their own feathers, must again build up their body reserves. Selecting the site and building the nest, laying the eggs and incubating them, and rearing the downy young until they are capable of flying many hours nonstop must all be done in the incredible time of approximately 110 days!

In the fall these birds, having completed the reproductive cycle, accurately retrace the same migratory air lanes — their numbers greatly increased (if conditions have been favorable) by their immature offspring. This time, to most of us, they accentuate the melancholy feeling of another year gone by and the imminence of winter. Again, we are envious and wish we could accompany them to their more temperate wintering grounds.

Most humans see only the esthetic side of the fall migration. From the bird's standpoint, the return flight from the nesting grounds is a much more serious business than the northward migration. This time, the adult birds with their offspring, who are wary by intuition only — not experience — must face all of the natural hazards plus the long gauntlet of hunters throughout most of the trip. They must stop more often so that the young birds with less endurance can rest and feed and, at a large number of these stops, their welcome will be in the form of No. 6 shot. Many of the immature birds, along with a fewer number of adults, will never see their wintering quarters. Thanks to recent conservation programs, many of the surviving waterfowl will find refuges where they can wait out the hunting season or a least take advantage of the protected areas during their resting periods. Within a matter of days after the hunting season closes, these birds will leave the sanctuaries, spread out over their respective wintering grounds, and again start preparing for another generation.

Probably the most remarkable adaptation of all is the adjustment waterfowl have made to the ever increasing presence of man. In addition to facing all their natural enemies including predators, storms, and drought, they have been slaughtered by every possible means, robbed of their breeding and nesting grounds, subjected to pollution of their waters by industrial wastes and oil spills, and poisoned by lead shot and insecticides. In spite of all these monumental adversities, they have persevered — only their numbers have changed. Their great beauty, grace, intelligence, and most admirable life style remain unaltered. In many ways, to paraphrase the words of Kortright, our wonderful waterfowl could serve as a model for mankind.

A few of the 1,500,000 waterfowl using the sanctuary of Gray Lodge Refuge in the Sacramento Valley of California.

PART I
DABBLING DUCKS

These surface-feeding ducks, almost always found on fresh water, have a number of important characteristics that separate them from their diving cousins. One of the most obvious of these differences is the manner by which they obtain food. Instead of reaching their food source by diving, they normally prefer to feed by tipping or dabbling along the edges of small, shallow bodies of water, preferably ones with a good cover of grasses or reeds. In the fall, a large amount of their food is gotten from harvested grain and cornfields where they relish the ripened kernels left by machines and animals. Regardless of whether they feed in the water or on land, most of their food is vegetable matter, and they are generally considered the most edible of all the ducks. Dabblers, or puddle ducks as they are sometimes called, constitute our most important group of ducks.

Compared to diving ducks, the legs of puddle ducks are placed farther forward and closer together and their feet are smaller — features that enable them to ambulate more freely. As a result, they are much more at home on land than the divers. Unlike the divers, their hind toe has no flap or lobe (see page 86). The dabbling ducks are excellent swimmers and can dive adeptly if the necessity arises. Diving as a means of escape is usually restricted to times when they are incapable of flight.

With bodies normally parallel to the ground, the stance of dabbling ducks is very similar to geese. Ducks of this group float buoyantly in the water with their tails normally held well above and at an angle to the surface, a posture again quite similar to geese.

Dabbling ducks, like other waterfowl, are strong, fast flyers of great endurance. For their weight, they generally have larger wings (usually rather long and pointed) and fly with much less effort and possess a great deal more maneuverability than diving ducks. They are capable of leaping directly into the air from either land or water, a feat requiring tremendous power. When taking off from water, the initial impetus is supplied by the first powerful downstroke of their outstretched wings striking the water. With the exception of the bufflehead, and possibly the hooded merganser, all other waterfowl require a running take off into the wind in order to gain flying speed. The flight speed of the dabbling ducks is normally considered to be somewhat slower than that of some of the divers. Accurate determination of the flight speed of birds is difficult and can only be done with any degree of accuracy from an airplane or helicopter inasmuch as this method of flight speed determination eliminates the effect of wind. As more checks are made by means of aircraft, it may be determined that the flight speed of the pintail and the teal is comparable to the canvasback, now considered to be the fastest of the ducks.

Dabblers are usually quite gregarious and are often seen in flocks, both on land and on water. Group flights are occasionally made in a V formation, but more often with no particular pattern. Almost all of the male ducks in this group have distinctively marked, brightly colored plumage. Except for the black duck and wood duck species, the female dabbling ducks are all quite similarly marked and colored. The plumage of the female black duck resembles the male very closely, while the female wood duck, although quite differently marked and colored from her mate, is the only native female duck whose plumage, other than the speculum, has iridescent coloring.

It is generally believed that ducks take a different mate each year. In captivity, ducks are actually quite faithful and seldom take a new mate if the old one is available. Eventually, it may be ascertained that more wild ducks breed with their former mates than is now known. Because of the male ducks' habit of generally leaving the females and banding together during the summer and autumn months, there is obviously less chance of their becoming reunited. However, many female ducks have been known to return to the exact same spot each year for nesting. It does not seem to be completely impossible that the male might return to the same general vicinity even though the pair had been separated after the previous breeding season.

Comparative profiles of dabbling ducks and diving ducks.

I–1   Common mallard, male (Chap. 1).   I–2   Black duck (Chap. 2).

I–3   Common mallard, female (Chap. 1).

I–4   Northern pintail, male and female (Chap. 3).   I–5

I–6   American widgeon, male, preening (Chap. 4).   I–7   American widgeon, pair.

4   DABBLING DUCKS

I–8   Wood ducks, males (Chap. 6).

I–9   Wood duck, female.

I–10   Gadwall, pair (Chap. 5).

I–11   Green-winged teal, pair (Chap. 7).

I–12   Cinnamon teal, male (Chap. 8).

I–13   Blue-winged teal, male (Chap. 9).

I–14   Northern shoveler, male (Chap. 10).

I–15   Northern Shoveler, female.

6   DABBLING DUCKS

CHAPTER 1

Common Mallard

Anas platyrhynchos platyrhynchos

One of my fondest memories as a youth in North Dakota was seeing the thousands of migrating mallards that stopped at the lake on our farm and spent the evenings and nights feeding upon the harvested grain and cornfields. These birds arrived fairly late in the fall. Although the majority left before the first snowfall, some stayed either until the ice finally encompassed the whole lake, or a driving blizzard forced them to warmer lands.

The wild mallard drake in full breeding plumage can hardly be called "common." Were it not for the abundance and promiscuity of his domesticated or semidomesticated brothers in parks and barnyards, he would surely rate as one of the most handsome waterfowl next to the wood duck. One of the most beautiful sights I can recall is a male mallard coming in to land from directly overhead and away. The blue-violet iridescence of his magnificient black and white bordered speculums highlighted on outstretched wings; a highly iridescent, green head flashing brilliantly in the sunlight; the expanded whitish tail extending from a glossy black rump, glistening with green iridescence, and further adorned with two tail coverts curled upwards into a ringlet; fully exposed scapulars and tertials delicately shading from dark brown to light, brownish gray; and the already splendidly colored plumage given accent by a yellow bill and orange feet are but some of the vivid impressions that come quickly to mind. (Color photos I-1 and 3, page 3.)

Mallards are the best known and most widespread of all the ducks, and they have adapted themselves to man better than any other species. They breed over a large range, covering most of the northwestern part of this continent, and winter in practically all but the north central states and the west coast of Canada. There is hardly any place in the United States and Canada where mallards are not seen at least some time during the year. Female mallards almost always nest on the ground fairly close to a pothole or a slough, although at times they will nest at considerable distances from water, and have been known to nest on the roof of a building. Mallards are prolific ducks under normal conditions and are probably more prone to hybridism than any other duck species.

The eclipse molt of the male mallard is complete, and thus very similar to the female. One distinguishing feature is his bill, which becomes a dull olive green without spotting, as compared to the orange, or greenish, spotted bill of the female.

Structurally, mallards are identical to black ducks; therefore, these photos can supplement those in Chapter 2 for body shape and position.

1–1 The handsome mallard drake in breeding plumage. Observe profile shape of body, expecially in flank area, and fore-and-aft positioning of legs (tarsi).

1–2 Body shape, position of crossed primaries, large tertials, and scapulars are shown in this view.

1–3 Note cross-sectional shape of crown and cheeks of this mallard drake's head.

1–4 Two drakes promenade with the females.

1-5 Drake in feeding position with legs widely spread. The cross-sectional shape of flank-rump area is round.

1-6 Three-quarter rear view showing additional body shape details.

1-7 Note triangular shape of back feather group. The large tertials do not always completely cover the wing.

1–8 Front, rear, and profile views of a pair of mated mallards. Take special note of tarsi placement.

1–9

1–10

1–11 Good profile view of a semialert mallard drake.

1–12 The changes in cross-sectional body shape are clearly shown in this rear view of a swimming drake.

1–13 Three-quarter rear and front views of an 1–14 alert drake.

1–15 A handsome drake tidies up his plumage.

1–16 This drake preens his head feathers by rubbing them against his partially expanded wing.

1–17 He continues by preening and oiling the feathers on the underside of his right wing.

1–18 The duck's flexible neck permits him to reach all parts of his body. Note position of tail.

1–19 He completes his toilet by preening his breast feathers.

1–20 Mated mallards relax in the sun and preen their feathers—a task that consumes much of their time.

1–21

Female mallard in feeding position. Profile and cross-sectional shape of body, location of tarsi—both fore-and-aft and laterally—position and shape of crossed primaries and tertials, and feather shape and markings are some of the structural details that can be obtained from these views.

1-24 Female mallard with partially exposed left wing and expanded tail. Note overlapping of tertials and scapulars. Also observe position of wing primaries, secondaries, and coverts.

1-25 Considerable plumage detail—both feather shape and markings—can be obtained from this photo.

1–26

1–27

This hen mallard industriously preens her wing feathers.

1–28

1–29

1–30 Good profile study of female mallard.

A few of the many flight positions of mallards.

CHAPTER 2

Black Duck

Anas rubripes

The impressive but somber-colored black duck may not be as beautiful, but he equals or surpasses his mallard cousin in every other way. Black ducks are considered the most intelligent, the wariest, and the wildest of all the ducks — they are ever on the alert and are rarely taken by surprise. Even in captivity, "blacks" retain their inborn distrust of man, quite unlike the easily domesticated common mallard.

Black ducks are by far the most numerous dabbling species in the eastern half of this country. Their breeding range covers eastern Canada and the northeastern United States. Early migrators, they start their southward flights during the first part of September and reach their favorite wintering grounds by late fall, some of them going as far south as Florida. However, many winter in parts of the New England states and as far north as Nova Scotia, where they are eventually forced to the coastal areas when the inland ponds and lakes become frozen. These birds, especially during the hunting season, spend their days on the salt water or inaccessible mud flats and feed at night in the salt marshes or nearby grainfields. Marine life, such as shellfish and crustaceans, abounds in these waters; as a result, blacks tend to eat more animal matter during the winter months than their mallard counterparts.

The coloration and markings of the female black duck closely resembles the male in breeding plumage with the following exceptions: the female's chest feathers have pointed V-shaped, buff-colored markings (markings on the male's side feathers are more rounded or U-shaped); their bills are shorter and are greener or more olive-yellow than the male's; and the color of their feet tends to be more brownish. The coloration of immature birds of both sexes resembles fairly closely that of the adult female, except their side feathers are widely edged with buff and lack the V-shaped markings. (Color photo I-2, page 3.)

Because of color variations of the bills and feet and other characteristics of black ducks, some naturalists formerly believed there were two distinct subspecies — the common black duck and the red-legged black duck. After more exhaustive studies, it was conceded by most that these variations in coloration and characteristics were attributable to sex, degree of maturity, and differences caused by the two molts.

Inasmuch as the plumage coloration and markings are essentially the same for both sexes, changes in the male's plumage brought about by the eclipse molt are very minor. Probably the most noticeable feature is the change in color of the bill from a yellow, or orange-yellow, to a dull olive green.

18

2–1 A fine black duck preens his back feathers. Note head and neck lines and raised primaries supporting his large tertial feathers.

2–2　Head and neck contours can be obtained from this picture. Observe intersection of scapulars and side feathers.

2–3　Good profile study of a relaxed black duck.

2–4 Drake raises his right wing while preening his back feathers.

2–5 Cross-sectional body shape and arrangement of primaries, tertials, and scapulars can be seen here.

2–6 Three blacks pose for the camera.

2–7 Striding black duck. Note position of feet and tarsi.

2–8   Profile and three-quarter rear view of semialert black ducks.   2–9

22–10   Studies of different head positions.   2–11

2–12   Pair of blacks dabble in quiet waters.

2–13   Three very relaxed black ducks. Note head positions and shapes.

CHAPTER 3

Northern Pintail

Anas acuta acuta

In flight, on the ground, or on the water, the northern pintail with his long, slim neck, streamlined body, and delicate, elongated tail is the most graceful of all ducks. These attributes, plus his strikingly handsome coloration and markings, make the elegant pintail a popular subject for paintings and carvings. The popularity of the pintail among hunters is second only to that of the mallard and the black duck. (Color photos I-4 and 5, page 4.)

Pintails, or "sprigs," as they are often called, are widely distributed throughout the Northern Hemisphere and have the greatest breeding range of the ducks of this continent. They also may be the most numerous — certainly second only to the mallard. Pintails are early migrants, starting their northward movement to the northern and western United States and all of Canada and Alaska around the middle of January. The females are often nesting in April, even in northern Alaska. Delacour reports that nests in California have been found at elevations as great as 8,400 feet. Hen pintails are among the bravest of all ducks, and are fearless in the defense of their young.

Prenuptial displays are performed on the water and also in the air. Two or more drakes vie for the attention of a female by raising their long necks to the fullest extent and pointing their bills downward against their chests and with their long tails pointed upwards. Eventually, the hen takes off followed by a drake, and they fly back and forth at full speed. The chase is usually joined by several more drakes and continues until all but one, possibly the original drake, have dropped out. The conjugal agreement having been completed, the pair settle back down on the water.

Pintails are the easiest to recognize of the waterfowl. Even when their colors and markings are not readily discernible, they are easily identified in the air by their slender, streamlined forms, wing beat, and long, narrow wings; and on the water by their graceful, distinctive profiles and upward slant of their long tails.

When on the water, pintails are seemingly always on the alert. If alarmed, they extend their long necks straight up to gain visibility. Should flight be necessary, they leap vertically from the water with powerful wing strokes. They are swift, strong, agile flyers with amazing endurance. Groups coming into land from great heights lose altitude at a steep angle and at high velocities, often by slipping with outspread, fixed wings positioned almost vertically to the ground, first one way and then the other in a zigzag motion. These are breathtaking and beautiful maneuvers to witness, and the sound of air rushing through crackling pinions can be heard for a considerable distance.

During the eclipse molt, pintail drakes closely resemble the hens, but can be easily distinguished by their larger size.

3–1 The magnificent pintail drake in full breeding plumage. When used in conjunction with photo 3–3, the shape and location of the primaries, tertials, and scapulars can be accurately determined.

3–2 Male in semialert position. Pintails are the most streamlined of all the ducks.

3–3 Cross-sectional body shape and lateral location of legs can be determined from this view.

3–4 Notice how primaries are raised when the bird is in a feeding position.

3–5 Pintail drake with primaries of left wing partially raised and tail expanded. 3–6

3–7 Female in classic sleeping position. Male has awakened and keeps a watchful eye on author.

3–8 Drake preens his breast feathers. Note location of white stripes on head and neck.

3–9 A drake pintail in a hurry—full stride.

3–10 Profile of a drake in an alert position.

3–11　Good profile views of the immaculately dressed male pintail.　3–12

3–13　These two pintail drakes are walking in a normal manner. They are very much at home on land.　3–14

3–15　Observe change of body shape in flank and belly area.

3–16　Pintail drake resting but still completely alert.

3-17   Striding pintail pair about to enter the water.

3–18 Female pintail in feeding position. Take particular note of the leg positions.

3–19 Hen pintail about to take a step.

3–20 Body shape and lateral position of legs can be determined from this view.

3–21 This pintail hen has raised her scapulars, exposing wing secondaries and coverts.

3–22 Interesting studies of the beautiful little female. 3–23

3–24 Female pintail in a standing, relaxed pose. Excellent view for establishing profile head and body shape.

3–25　Front and rear views showing head and neck contours and body shape.　3–26

3–27　Striding female. She has been pinioned and is not as trim as a flying bird.

3–28　A lovely little hen in a semialert pose.

3–29 The graceful, delicate lines of the pintail drake are very evident in this photograph.

3–30 Profile and rear views of a swimming female. 3–31

3–32 A mated pair of pintails take a leisurely swim.

3-33   Two males displaying to impress a rather indifferent female.

3-34   Another pair of males view for the attentions of a demure hen.

3-35   This drake proudly shows off his new bride.

3-36   Profile studies of a male and female pintail. The hen is alert and ready for instant flight.   3-37

3–38 Five drakes try to win attention of single female during courtship flight.

3–39 Pintails are graceful and powerful flyers. 3–40

CHAPTER 4

American Widgeon

Anas americana

The delightful, saucy, and feisty widgeons breed exclusively in North America. Commonly called baldpates, they resemble quite closely the European widgeon, a fairly common visitor to both coasts. Widgeons are not only beautifully colored and marked, they are active, distinctive, alert birds who sit gracefully on the water with their tails held high. Seldom still, they pivot often as they peck daintily for food, the iridescent green head patches of the drakes flashing brilliantly in the sunlight. The male talks with a low, soft whistle, usually repeated three times in quick succession. In direct contrast, the female's call is a most unmusical croak. (Color photos I-6 and 7, page 4.)

Widgeons are very much at home on the land, where their grazing habits resemble geese and their trotting movements resemble pigeons. They are very fond of wild celery and eelgrass roots and are often seen on tidal flats partaking of this delicacy. During high tides, when the eelgrass is flooded, these sometime brigands resort to more devious means of obtaining their favorite food. Inept at the art of diving, baldpates generously permit canvasbacks and redheads, sometimes even coot, to bring up the succulent morsels and, during the dive, position themselves at the proper spot to relieve these unsuspecting waterfowl of their hard-won gains. However, widgeons probably more than repay these divers for their efforts by serving as sentinels, and are quick to loudly quack the alarm and flush if danger is imminent. When frightened, they leap vertically from the water in disorder with a loud clattering noise and fly away, turning and twisting and grouped so closely together that it seems impossible for them to move their wings without interfering with other flashing pinions.

In their natural habitat, widgeons are normally very nervous and wary, more so than most ducks; it is, therefore, strange that a fair number inhabit small park-type ponds during the winter months, exhibit very little fear of humans, and are quite willing to accept food, almost out of the hand.

Widgeons breed in the north central states, central Canada, and Alaska. They winter from Vancouver down through Central America on the west, from Cape Cod to the West Indies on the east, and across the southern part of the United States.

When the male acquires his eclipse plumage, he resembles the female, except for his wings which have renewed their completely white wing patches.

4–1   Feisty widgeon drake hurls insults at an intruder. Excellent profile of a threatening pose.

4–2 Alert female widgeon is suspicious of author's gunlike telephoto lens. Note shape and position of her primaries, tertials, and scapulars. Good profile view of head.

4–3 Striding widgeon drake. Note intersection of scapulars and side feathers.

4–4 Well-fed drake displays his smooth, streamlined body.

4–5 Cross-sectional body shape and lateral location of legs can be ascertained from these two views. 4–6

4–7 Preening drake. Observe position of the primaries of his left wing.

4–8 This drake is carefully arranging his wing covert feathers.

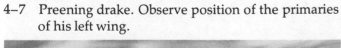

4-9

4-10

Position and shape of wing primaries, beautifully marked tertials, and scapulars are quite evident in these views of a preening widgeon drake.

4-11

4-12

4–13 This view of a stepping drake is helpful in establishing cross-sectional body shape.

4–14 Drake in an interesting, crouching pose.

4–15 Good profile of a widgeon drake. Fore-and-aft leg location can also be determined here.

4–16 This drake alertly watches author.

4–17 Striding and alert baldpate drake. By muscular control of feathers, he changes overall shape of his head. The white wing patch is often visible when their wings are folded.   4–18

4–19   An alert mated pair of widgeon. These birds are ready to take wing.

4–20   In addition to head and bill shape, a great deal can be learned from this photo about the shape, location, and markings of this hen widgeon's upper feathers.

4–21 Hen widgeon in classic wing- and leg-stretching pose. Note position of right leg and foot.

4–22 Preening female. Observe cross-sectional body shape and lateral position of legs.

4–23 Female widgeon in neck-stretching positions. 4–24

4–25 Hen widgeon in a good feeding pose. Particularly note position of legs.

4–26   Alert female rests daintily on the water.

4–27   Hen widgeon in a more relaxed pose.

4–28   Drake dabbles for feed in the water.

4–29   This male widgeon is preening his breast feathers.

4–30   Drake in a semialert position. Notice how iridescent green head patches extend down neck.

4–31   Excellent profile view of splendid widgeon drake.

4–32   This little female is in a completely relaxed pose.

4–33   Mated pair of widgeons float lazily in the water.

4–34   The beautifully marked and colored widgeon drake is truly a handsome bird.

4–35

Widgeons are excellent flyers and are capable of spectacular maneuvers.

4–36

CHAPTER 5

Gadwall

Anas strepera

The male gadwall, although beautiful in his own subdued way, is the least colorful of the dabbling ducks. Mainly because of his rather drab plumage coloration, gadwalls are more often incorrectly identified than any of the other duck species. When on the water and at a distance, they appear to be medium size, grayish-brown ducks with somewhat lighter heads and necks. In the eastern part of the country and in marginal light, gadwalls are sometimes mistaken for black ducks. They are often seen in the company of pintails and widgeons and are commonly confused with hen pintails and immature male pintails. In the air, their bodies are slender and their wing beat is similar to pintails, which again causes misidentification. Both the drake and the hen gadwall have a singular feature — they are the only dabbling ducks to have white speculums. Actually, their inner secondary feathers are white, the middle secondary feathers are black, and the outer secondary feathers are grayish with white tips. When viewed at close range or in the hand, the distinctive marking and coloration of gadwalls are quite obvious — there is little excuse for improper identification. (Color photo I-10, page 5.)

The gadwall has a wide distribution throughout the Northern Hemisphere. It is found in almost all regions except in South America and Australia. Its distribution in North America, however, is smaller than most dabbling ducks, and its breeding range is generally restricted to the prairie regions of northwestern United States and southwestern Canada.

Records of banded birds indicate that the central prairie-raised birds winter in the Mississippi Valley and along the Gulf Coast and into Mexico, while the birds raised in western Canada, Washington, and Oregon winter in central California. Gadwalls prefer mild weather and are one of the earliest species to start their southward migration in the fall and one of the latest to head north in the spring, usually waiting until the ice has melted from their favorite ponds. They are venturesome ducks and, like mallards, adapt quickly to newly created habitats.

One of the important characteristics of dabbling ducks which separates them from the diver group is that they obtain their food by tipping and dabbling. As so often happens when generalizations are made, exceptions occur. Kortright states, "The gadwall is one of the few surface-feeding ducks that can and does dive for food, though this habit is only indulged in when absolutely necessary; it usually feeds by dabbling in marshes and sloughs."

The eclipse plumage of the male is complete, except his chest feathers are more finely marked. His bill is similar to the female, but is not spotted.

5–1

5–2

Although his colors are subdued, the gadwall drake is a finely marked and elegant duck.

5-3   A beautiful pair of mated gadwall. This picture, taken in March, portrays these birds in their finest plumage.

5–4 A gadwall drake meticulously preens and oils his wing feathers.

5–5 An excellent view for determining body shape.

5–6 A gadwall drake swims toward the camera. Note position and shape of crossed primaries and tertials.

5–7　The beautifully marked breast feathers of the male gadwall are very evident in this photograph.

5–8　Gadwall drake takes a nap.

5–9

5–10

5–11　Rear view of a pinioned gadwall drake. Note head shape and expanded tail.

5–12　Pinioned birds are often not as trim as free-flying birds because of their less strenuous lives.

5–13   The female gadwall in many ways resembles the female mallard.

5–14   A fine pair of mated gadwalls.

CHAPTER 6

Carolina Wood Duck

Aix sponsa

Carolina wood ducks, the most beautiful of all waterfowl, are strictly a North American species and, in addition, their natural range is almost completely confined to the contiguous United States. There are two separate populations; the larger is located in the eastern half of the United States, extending a short distance into southeastern Canada; the other group is found in the Pacific Northwest, extending from southwestern British Columbia south into the San Joaquin Valley of California.

Words cannot adequately describe the male wood duck's exquisite markings and rich, iridescent plumage whose brilliant colors span the full range of the spectrum. Even the hen wood duck is more colorful than the females of the other duck species, and she is the only one to possess a considerable amount of iridescent plumage. (Color photos I-8 and 9, page 5.)

Because of his great beauty and tasty flesh, the wood duck was overhunted in the early days. In addition, logging of the woodland swamps reduced greatly the number of big, hollow tree trunks required by wood ducks for nesting sites. As a result, this species was on the verge of extinction. Fortunately for all bird lovers, regulatory steps were taken in time by both the United States and Canada and the hunting of wood ducks was prohibited from 1918 until 1941. Due to the continuance of good conservation methods and the provision of many nesting boxes and artificial ponds, the wood duck has again become a fairly common species in many areas. Also, many wood ducks are now being hand-raised and released in areas where they were scarce or never existed, thereby not only increasing their numbers but also their breeding range.

The courtship ritual of the male wood duck is simple, usually consisting of bowing and the emittance of low, whistling calls. Once the female has accepted her mate, she leads him back into the woodlands searching for a nesting site, usually in the area where she was hatched or had previously nested. The tree cavity selected is more often than not some distance from the ground or water, sometimes as much as 50 or 60 feet. In addition, the bottom of the cavity where the nest is located may be 6 or 8 feet below the opening. If it is difficult to visualize how the female can make a vertical ascent in such a limited space, it is much harder to understand how the two-day-old babies could possibly climb to the opening. As usual, nature has wonderfully provided the necessary means—the downy young when hatched have needle-sharp claws and a hooked nail at the tip of the bill that enables them to climb up the sides of the cavity. Many people in recent years have watched the baby wood ducks, when called by their mother, leap from the cavity opening and float down to the ground safely. However, Arthur Cleveland Bent (*Life Histories of North American Waterfowl*) quotes three different writers who witnessed female wood ducks physically carry their young, one at a time, down from the cavity opening to the ground.

6–1 The most beautiful of all waterfowl—the Carolina wood duck drake. His rich, iridescent colors and exquisite markings are almost indescribable.

6–2 Good front view showing body shape and leg placement.

6–3 His left wing is partially exposed as he has just stopped preening it.

6–4 Wood duck drake with his left wing exposed and his scapular raised.

6–5 The magnificent drake poses in an alert position. Good view for establishing head and body shape and leg location.

6–6 Preening poses. Note expanded tail. 6–7

6–8   Striding woodie. Almost on the verge of extinction at the turn of the century, they have now made a strong comeback and are quite plentiful in many parts of the country.

6–9   In these studies, note shape of crest feathers and chest-neck lines.   6–10

6–11 Resting female wood duck. Although not quite as colorful as her illustrious mate, she is the only female duck with a considerable amount of iridescent colors. She is an elegant bird in every respect.

6–12

6–13

Studies of a resting wood duck hen. Note location of her supporting foot and leg relative to her body.

6–14

6–15

6-16 Wood ducks ride quite buoyantly on the water with tail and wing primaries normally held high.

6-17

6-18

More pictorial studies of woodies on the water.

6-19

6-20

6-21

Mated pair of wood ducks loaf under a flowered bush.

6-22

6-23   Hen wood duck in a semialert pose.

6-24   This little hen is about to take a nap.

6–25   Three-quarter rear and profile of hen wood ducks.   6–26

6–27   Female rests on one leg. Note position of right foot.

6–28   She now stands on both feet—note partially exposed wing and expanded tail.

6–29   Studies of a preening female wood duck.   6–30

CHAPTER 7

Green-Winged Teal

Anas crecca

As Kortright so appropriately wrote, "The drake green-winged teal, in the eyes of many, ranks second only to the gorgeous wood duck. A wealth of delicate loveliness is blended on the tiny person of this, the smallest of waterfowl." Another writer described these beautiful ducks as resembling little porcelain birds.

The green-winged teal is almost identical with his cousin, the European teal. The latter lacks the white crescent on the side of the body forward of the wing. The outer scapulars of the European teal are edged with white and black, forming a white and black line on both sides of the body. The long scapulars of the green-winged teal are edged with black only. One other minor difference is that the iridescent green head patch on the European teal is bordered top and bottom with a light buff-colored line. On the greenwing, the green head patch is bordered only on the lower side. The females of the two are indistinguishable. (Color photo I-11, page 4.)

The green-winged teal have a wide distribution — they breed in most of the northern half of this continent, but more sparingly in the eastern part. Although the breeding range of the green-winged teal extends much farther north of that of the blue-winged teal, the center of the nesting population is in the pothole areas of the northern states and the southwestern half of Canada. Southward migration starts with the first cold weather and some of these ducks, the hardiest of the three indigenous teal species, winter as far north as British Columbia in the west and southern New England in the east. However, the main wintering population is in the southern states and Mexico.

The green-winged teal is one of the earlier migrants in the spring, following pintails and mallards closely. They start leaving the southern boundaries of their wintering range as early as February and work slowly northward, some reaching their breeding areas in Alaska in May. Most birds are paired during the leisurely migration and start nesting immediately upon reaching their individual nesting areas. Incubation and the raising of the young falls entirely upon the tiny female, the smallest of all ducks, who performs her tasks with the utmost devotion. The plumage of young feathered birds is very similar to the female, except the colors are duller. By December, the young birds have matured and their plumage is almost identical to older birds.

Like the other teals, greenwings are great flyers and may be one of the fastest ducks, although their small size probably tends to create an illusion of a higher speed than they are actually maintaining. They are very much at home on land and walk easily and gracefully and can run quite swiftly. On the water, they are excellent swimmers and can dive proficiently if necessary for escape.

7–1   The exquisite little green-winged teal drake in a relaxed pose. He is the smallest of our waterfowl, but one of the most beautiful.

7–2   The little male spruces up his feathers.   7–3

7–4 Another study of the male greenwing. Drakes habitually hold their heads close to their bodies.

7–5 Mated pair of greenwings. Female preens her chest feathers.

7–6 Greenwing drake in an interesting pose.

7–7 The greenwing hen is even smaller than her mate.

7–8 Tiny hen in feeding pose—note marking of back and scapular feathers.

7–9 Good profile of drake.

7–10 Mated pair relax in the sun.

7–11 Male stretching leg. Note expanded tail.

7–12 After stretching, he resumes his relaxed pose.

7–13   Little female poses for picture.

7–14   Nice pose. Note prominence of upper side feathers.

7–15   She displays her scapulars, tertials, and side feathers. Observe how the feathers over her rump
are raised.

7–16   Mated pair loaf in the quiet waters.

7–17   Tiny hen arranges her side feathers.

7–18   Good profile of the floating female.

7–19   Female greenwing takes a nap.

7–20   Note prominent scapular and tertial feathers.

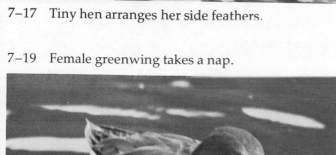

67

7–21 Observe drake's head and bill shape—also note conspicuous back feather group.

7–22

7–23

More studies of the green-winged teal drake.

7–24

7–25

68

CHAPTER 8

Northern Cinnamon Teal

Anas cyanoptera septentrionalium

It was formerly believed that northern cinnamon teal were the only dabbling duck species whose breeding and wintering range was confined to the North American continent. More recent studies indicate that some cinnamon teal migrate as far south as Colombia and Venezuela. Cinnamon teal are common west of the Rockies with their breeding range extending eastward to western Kansas and Texas and from British Columbia to western and central Mexico. It is therefore most unusual that this species was first recorded in Louisiana in 1849. There are two distinct populations of cinnamon teal in the Americas, the one referred to above and the other in the southern half of South America. These two groups are separated by 2,000 miles—there is no known migration between them.

Cinnamon and blue-winged teal are closely related; in fact, they both are more closely related to shovelers than they are to the other teals, not only in coloration and structure but also in feeding habits (see Chapter 10). Unless accompanied by the male of the species, identification of female cinnamon and blue-winged teal in the field is practically impossible. When birds in the hand are compared, there are small differences in bill shape and size (see Chapter 9). (Color photo I-12, page 6.)

These most colorful teal are early migrators—some starting their southward journey in early August. Cin-

namon teal, like blue-winged teal, are late in acquiring their breeding plumage. Although Bent states they acquire full breeding plumage by October or November, I have never seen a male cinnamon in breeding plumage with fully developed and colored scapulars until fairly late in December.

Most unusual among ducks, the male cinnamon does not always desert the female once incubation of the eggs has been started. Families of ducklings accompanied by both parents are seen on occasion; if danger is imminent, the male is the one more likely to show concern for the young. Cinnamon teal prefer to inhabit tule-bordered shallow lakes or marshes where the thick cover helps protect them from their enemies and provides them with food. These are not gregarious ducks — they seem to prefer to be alone with their mates or families.

Also like blue-winged teal, they are great flyers and possess incredible endurance. According to Paul A. Johnsgard, (*Waterfowl of North America*), an immature female was banded near Ogden, Utah, on July 31, and was recovered near Mexico City on August 15. This remarkable flight required an average daily movement of 114 miles.

The eclipse molt of the drake begins in June and is resembles the female, except his head and neck are more cinnamon-buff in coloration.

69

8–1 Canvasback hen in background dwarfs the beautiful little cinnamon teal drake.

8–2 Alert male and female cinnamon teal. Note large and beautifully marked scapulars and tertials on male.

8–3   Cinnamon teal are a little larger than green-winged teal. Their bills are considerably larger.

8–4   Sleepy cinnamon drake takes a sip of water.

8–5

8–6

Four photographic studies of a cinnamon teal hen.

8–7

8–8

8–9   A mated pair of cinnamon teal take a stroll in the afternoon sun.

72

8–10 A striding drake—good profile view. Drakes are late in getting their breeding plumage.

8–11 Three-quarter rear view showing shape and markings of scapular and tertial feathers.

8–12 Cinnamon teal drake takes a lunch break. 8–13

8–14 Resting cinnamon drake.

8–15 Front view showing head, bill, and body shape.

8–16　Two studies of an alert cinnamon drake.　8–17

8–18　　　　　　　　　　　　　　　　8–19

Cinnamon teal are slow to lose their distrust for man.

8–20

CHAPTER 9

Blue-Winged Teal

Anas discors

The blue-winged teal, plentiful in the east and interior, is another duck of the Americas. Unfortunately for Westerners, they are seldom seen on the Pacific Coast. Nature, however, has compensated for this apparent oversight by giving the West the beautiful, little cinnamon teal instead. Bluewings breed in most of the northern states and central Canada and winter in the southern states.

Although the male blue-winged teal is unmistakeably marked and colored, the female is almost identical to the female cinnamon teal. From a distance it is impossible to distinguish one from the other. As hybridism is rare among wild teal, the ducks themselves obviously have no identification problems. When identifying birds in the hand, the blue-winged female has a somewhat smaller bill of constant width. The cinnamon teal hen usually has a longer, wider bill that is slightly constricted in planform near its base. The female shoveler is of general coloration as the bluewing female, but the hen shoveler is easily identified, even from a distance, by her huge, spatulate bill. (Color photo I-13, page 4.)

The blue-winged teal is a late migrator in the spring, and some of them linger in the warm marshes of the southern areas of North America until May. Much of their courtship is performed on the wing; but one of its more interesting phases occurs on the water or on adjacent land. The male and female bow to each other every couple of seconds for a period of several minutes. This ritual is carried on for hours, interspersed with feeding and resting periods. Once the nuptial ties are bound, nesting and incubation begin in the usual manner, including desertion by the male. Once hatched, the young develop more rapidly than the large duck species and are generally able to fly in six weeks. By fall, the young acquire plumage quite similar but duller in color to the adult birds. Young males do not obtain their bright, breeding plumage and the beautiful blue edge on their long scapulars until their second year.

These little teal, like other teal, are strong, fast, and agile flyers of great endurance. Due to the fact that a large number of bluewings winter in South America, many long flights of banded birds have been recorded. One was banded at the Patuxent Wildlife Research Center in Maryland and six months later was taken in Sullana, Peru, an airline distance of 7,000 miles. Another was banded at the Delta Waterfowl Research Station in Manitoba, Canada, and was killed on a lake 13,000 feet above sea level near Quito, Ecuador. Still another bird was banded in Quebec, Canada, on September 5, 1930, and was shot on October 2, 1930, in British Guiana, a direct distance of 2,400 miles. This incredible flight required an average daily flight of 85 miles!

The eclipse plumage of the drake is complete, resembling closely that of the female. They are later than most ducks in acquiring their full breeding plumage, often not until January or February.

9–1 A beautiful mated pair of blue-winged teal dabble in warm waters.

9–2 Profile study of the blue-winged drake. Note large, beautifully marked tertials.

9–3 Blue-winged teal male in a semialert pose.

9–4   Pair of bluewings cruise slowly by.

9–5   Profile and rear view studies of a standing blue-winged drake.   9–6

9–7   Blue-winged drake relaxes in the sun. Good standing pose.

9–8   A little drake preens his strikingly marked scapulars.

9–9   Interesting studies of a blue-winged pair.   9–10
9–12

9–11   Another profile view of a bluewing drake.

9–13   Profile and front view studies of the hen.   9–14

CHAPTER　　　10

Northern Shoveler

Anas clypeata

Shovelers, or spoonbills as they are more commonly called, have a worldwide distribution. Their distribution in the United States is quite general; however, they are more abundant in the western and southern parts of the country. Their oversize spatulate bills make them one of the easiest of the ducks to identify under almost all conditions. As far as habits, plumage, coloration, and structure are concerned, shovelers are closely related to the blue-winged and cinnamon teals. The New Zealand shoveler has the crescent-shaped face patches of the blue-winged teal and the red shoveler of South America has the blue-winged teal body markings and coloration. The northern shoveler drake in breeding plumage is a most handsome bird and, despite his oversized bill, is an interesting and popular carving subject. (Color photos I-14 and 15, page 4.)

Prenuptial displays are carried out both in the air and on the water, but are relatively restrained in comparison to the other ducks. However, the mating arrangement of shovelers in some cases is quite unusual. In breeding areas where the sexes are approximately equal, the male and female ducks mate and keep together in the usual manner. In areas where males out-

number females, females occasionally accept the attentions of two males. Usually, the two adult birds pair off and the second drake, in almost all cases an immature bird, then appears on the scene. The immature drake has probably found that females his own age do not breed until the following season and he gratefully accepts the attention of the older and mated female. This triangular love affair apparently works out very smoothly and there is little, if any, rivalry between the two males. Mallard hens on occasion accept two males but there is normally considerable jealousy between them and brawls are common.

Shovelers are excellent flyers — they jump strongly from the ground or water straight up into the air and move out with a swift and somewhat erratic flight, resembling the flight of teal to a degree. Their endurance is also comparable to that of the blue-winged teal and they are one of the few ducks that make the 2,000-mile flight from Alaska to the Hawaiian Islands.

The eclipse plumage is acquired rapidly by the drake in June and closely resembles the female. The male's large, black bill assumes a yellowish-green color at this time.

10-1   Despite his large bill, the shoveler drake in breeding plumage is a most handsome bird.

10-2   Drake balances on one foot and scratches his head. See photo 10-5.

10-3　The shoveler's huge, spatulate bill is quite evident in these photos.　10-4

10-5　Head scratching as viewed from the other side.

10-6　Drake's oversize bill does not prevent him from keeping his plumage in perfect condition.

10–7 Mated pair of shovelers on the alert.

10–8 Good profile of a relaxed drake.

10–9 Drake in an unusual head high position.

10–10 This rear view clearly shows body and head shape.

10–11 Shoveler's beautiful scapulars and tertials are similar to the blue-winged and cinnamon teals.

10–12   Profile portrait of a shoveler hen. Her body markings and coloration are similar to the hen mallard.

10–13   Hen relaxes on smooth water. Her bill is well adapted for straining food from water and mud.

10–14   Body shape and feather detail are evident in this rear view of a pinioned female.

10–15   Mated pair about to go for a swim.

10–16   Shovelers are powerful, agile flyers.

PART II
DIVING DUCKS

The native diving ducks covered in this part have been classified by Delacour into four different groups: the pochard group (Tribe *Aythini*) which includes the canvasback, redhead, ring-necked duck, and greater and lesser scaup; the goldeneye, merganser, and scoter group (Tribe *Mergini*) of which only the harlequin, American and Barrow's goldeneyes, bufflehead, and the hooded merganser are included herein; the eider group (Tribe *somaterini*), and the stiff-tailed duck group (Tribe *Oxyorini*), represented here by the ruddy duck.

The pochards, by their general behavior, are more closely related to the dabbling ducks than are the other diving ducks. Coloration and markings of the downy young of these divers are quite similar to the young of the dabblers. Pochards are generally found on fresh water, although the redhead and greater scaup prefer coastal waters during the winter.

Goldeneyes and mergansers are even better divers than the pochards—some of them are actually capable of catching fish. Most spend their breeding period on or near fresh water. These ducks, with their large tails and similar nesting habits, are near relatives of the perching ducks, except they have adapted to underwater feeding. According to Delacour (1954), a mating of a female hooded merganser with a male wood duck, producing hybrid offspring, has been recorded.

The eider species (included by some in the *Mergini* Tribe) have some characteristics of the dabbling ducks during their breeding season but are strictly sea ducks the rest of the time. These are the hardiest of all waterfowl; their northern wintering range is limited only by the availability of open water.

The little ruddy duck of the stiff-tailed tribe is an excellent diver but is almost helpless on land. Ducks of this group closely represent the characteristics of grebes. As their tribe name implies, their tails are long and stiff—often held in the vertical position or even pointed toward their heads.

Diving ducks generally have short, heavy bodies, large heads, large feet, and most have small, short tails. Compared to dabblers, their legs are set farther back and are more widely spread—features which enable them to swim and dive exceptionally well, but hinder their movements on the ground. As a result, divers are uncomfortable on land and are rarely seen out of the water. Because of their rearward leg location, their bodies are usually held more upright when walking than surface feeding ducks. All of the diving ducks, including the ruddy duck, have large lobes or flaps on their hind toes which provide a positive means of identifying the divers from the dabblers (see page 86). Diving ducks normally float low in the water with their tails usually held parallel to the surface and often actually in the water. Their wings are smaller relative to their weight, and the wing beat is more rapid than the dabblers'; however, the flight of divers is strong, direct, and fast, but they do not possess the great maneuverability characteristic of the dabbling ducks. In flight, their large feet extend well beyond their short tails and are often used as rudders. Due to their smaller wings, diving ducks (buffleheads, hooded mergansers, and possibly harlequins excepted) are unable to spring into the air as dabbling ducks do. They require a running start, pattering along the surface of the water for some distance in order to gain flying speed.

Like the dabbling ducks, male divers desert their mates shortly after incubation is started. They then gather in large groups on open water and proceed to molt into their eclipse plumage. Unlike dabbling ducks, they do not seek concealment during their flightless period. Also similar to surface feeding ducks, female divers abandon their young some time before they are able to fly and resort to the marshes for protective cover during their flightless molting period.

The male and female divers are differently colored and marked. The females are uniformly brownish and lack the variegated and streaked markings of the female dabblers. All of the male divers covered herein, except the canvasback, have at least some iridescent coloring on their heads. The ring-necked drake is the only diver who has other iridescent coloring — his upper parts have a metallic green sheen. None of the divers of either sex has iridescent speculums.

Comparison of dabbling and diving ducks' feet. Note large lobe on hind toe of the canvasback's foot.

Canvasback.   Common Mallard.

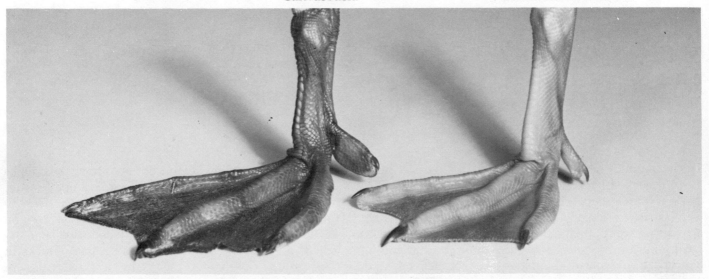

Little bufflehead drake plying his trade.

II–1   Redhead, male (Chap. 11).

II–2   Redhead, female.

II–3   Canvasback, male and female (Chap. 12).   II–4

II–5   Greater scaup, male and female (Chap. 13).   ·II–6

II–7   Harlequin duck (Chap. 15).

II–8   Ring-necked duck (Chap. 14).

II–9 Hooded mergansers, pair (Chap. 16).

II–10 Hooded merganser, male, displaying.

II–11 Bufflehead, male, stretching wings (Chap. 17).

II–12 American common eiders, pair (Chap. 18).

II–13   Ruddy duck, male, displaying (Chap. 21).

II–14   American goldeneye, male (Chap. 19).

II–15   Barrow's goldeneyes, pair (Chap. 20).

II–16   Barrow's goldeneyes.

CHAPTER 11

Redhead

Aythya americana

Ms. Redhead, the most liberated of the female ducks, is not one to wait demurely for the romantic attentions of the drakes—she has absolutely no inhibitions in taking the initiative during the mating rituals. Once mated, however, the drake employs disciplinary measures and wastes no time showing his once aggressive bride who wears the male feathers. Some of the females resent this roughshod treatment and show their independence by depositing their eggs in the nests of unsuspecting or less determined females of their own kind, or even in nests of canvasbacks, scaups, and ruddys—to name a few. Other less emancipated redhead females construct beautiful nests and dutifully incubate, hatch, and rear their brood, often very large—thanks to the generosity of their irresponsible sisters.

Redheads are often seen in the company of canvasbacks and scaups. Although these three diving duck species have some common features, the identification of the males, when on the water, should not be difficult. The coloration of the upper parts and sides of the redhead is similar but darker than the canvasback. Identification of the canvasback is made easy under almost all conditions by the very distinctive shape of his head, neck, and bill. The overall body coloration of the scaup is slightly darker than the canvasback but still is considerably lighter than the redhead. While the head and bill shape of the scaup and redhead are very similar, the prominent reddish, chestnut color of the latter's head makes identification relatively simple except in poor light conditions. Recognition of the females of these three species is more difficult. The female canvasback has the same head and bill shape of her mate, plus overall lighter body coloration than the female redhead—features which make her identification easy. Positive identification of the hen redhead and scaup is not as simple. Although the overall coloration of the female redhead is a little lighter than the female scaup, this feature usually does not provide sufficient means for identification. The white, or whitish, facial markings at the base of the bill is much more clearly defined on the female scaup and provides one of the better means of establishing identity. (Color photos 11-1 and 2, page 87.)

Redheads prefer open water and gather in "rafts" during the day, moving closer to shore to feed during the evening and early morning hours. Like canvasbacks, they are often robbed by widgeon and coots, but they take this thievery calmly in their stride and continue to dive until all are fed. The males have a most unusual call, one very similar to the meowing of a cat.

Their wintering area is large—from Oregon south into Mexico on the West Coast; and along the East Coast, from the Chesapeake Bay to Florida; along the Gulf Coast, and the West Indies. Their breeding range is much smaller, and includes the prairie pothole area of Canada and the United States, extending southwest to parts of Arizona.

11–1

Sleepy redhead drake. He is only slightly less impressive than the canvasback, and is a fine bird.

11–2

11–3   Classic redhead drake pose when on the water.

11–4   Another view of the sleepy redhead.

11–5 Swimming redhead male. Observe overlapping of the scapulars by the side feathers.

11–6 Two good standing poses for the redhead drake. 11–7

11–8 Three-quarter front and profile views of the redhead male. Note leg placement.   11–9

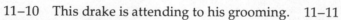

11–10   This drake is attending to his grooming.   11–11

11–12

11–13

Four interesting, typical diving duck poses.

11–14

11–15

11–16 Observe crossed primaries, tertials, and secondary wing feathers, also the separation of his side feathers.

11–17 Redhead drake touches oil gland with his bill prior to preening feathers.

11–18 Note how he has raised his scapular feathers, exposing wing coverts.

11–19 He raises his left wing to smooth down his rumpled covert feathers.

11–20   Same head position viewed from the front and from the side.   11–21

11–22 Frontal view of redhead hen. Cross-sectional body shape is shown quite clearly.

11–23 Female redhead preens her scapulars.

11–24   Hen reaches up with her foot and scratches her head.

11–25   Two studies of a sleepy hen. She has her bill tucked under her scapulars.   11–26

11-27

11-28

Four profile studies of standing poses.

11-29

11-30

11-31 Redhead hen takes it easy.

11-32 Another study of a hen preening.

11-33   Female redhead continues with her primping.   11-34

11-35   Two more studies of the standing female redhead.   11-36

CHAPTER 12

Canvasback

Aythya valisineria

The distinctive, kingly canvasback is still another exclusively North American species. In the eyes of sportsmen, artists, and bird watchers, he is the most highly regarded of all the ducks.

In the early years, canvasbacks wintered by the hundreds of thousands on the East Coast in the brackish waters of the bays and inlets and fed upon wild celery roots. Gourmets prized the flesh of the "can" over all waterfowl and its fame grew, probably out of proportion, until these ducks were hunted mercilessly for the market by every possible means. As a result of the great hunting pressure of former years and, in more recent years, the reduction of suitable nesting areas caused by drought and drainage of prairie potholes by man, plus the pollution of the bird's wintering waters, the splendid canvasback is no longer plentiful. Since 1960, hunting this species has either been illegal or the bag limit was reduced to one bird, two at the most. Even with this reduced hunting and with ample rainfall for the past three or four years in the nesting areas, canvasbacks have failed to multiply. It is hoped that more will be learned soon about this fine duck and his habitats so that better conservation methods can reverse the declining population trend.

Although the canvasback is certainly not the most beautiful from the standpoint of plumage coloration and markings, he has certain outstanding attributes. As Major Allan Brooks (*Natonal Geographic* magazine, Oc-

tober, 1934) wrote, "Aside from its reputation as a table delicacy, there is something regal and outstanding about the canvasback. All of its actions are full of character. The big, white body that seems to sit so high on the water, surmounted by the slender-shaped head on the long, thick neck, forms a striking picture. But when the flock is in full flight the big birds are seen at their best. There is such power expressed in the speed and directness of their driving flight, usually made in line formation, that it seems to stamp the 'can' as a superduck wherever he is found." (Color photos II-3 and 4, page 87.)

Canvasbacks breed in central Alaska and the prairie regions of the United States and Canada. They are hardy ducks, heading south in the fall only when their favorite ponds or lakes have frozen over. They migrate in large V-shaped flocks. Birds of the western breeding area winter along the Pacific Coast from southern British Columbia to central Mexico, while the birds breeding in the eastern portions of their range head for the Atlantic Coast and the coasts of the Gulf States. They are considered to be one of the faster, if not the fastest, flyers of all the ducks—flight speeds of over 70 mph have been recorded.

The eclipse molt of the canvasback is not as complete as most ducks and only lasts for a short time. By the first of November, the male bird is in his full breeding plumage.

12–1 The regal canvasback drake shows off his distinctive profile. Divers usually stand somewhat more erect than this.

12–2 Note head and neck shape of this relaxed canvasback male.

12–3 Drake preens head feathers by rubbing them against his wing.

12–4 Drake striding. Large feet and short, rearward located legs prevent his walking gracefully.

12–5 Canvasback drake in classic pose of a diver.

12–6 Cross-sectional body shape can be determined from this front view.

12–7   Canvasbacks seem to float more buoyantly than other divers. Note bill detail near its base.

12–8   This out-of-focus picture was included to show the heavy, straight-sided neck shape of an alert can.

12–9   Particularly observe body shape, tertials, and scapulars of this resting canvasback male.

12–10 Good profile view of the lordly canvasback.

12–11   Different head positions are shown in these two views. Take note of their heavy necks.   12–12

12–13   Note crossed primaries, tertials, and scapular feather groups. Also note cross-sectional body shape.   12–14

12–15   Strong character and lordly bearing are reflected in the canvasback drake's every position and movement.

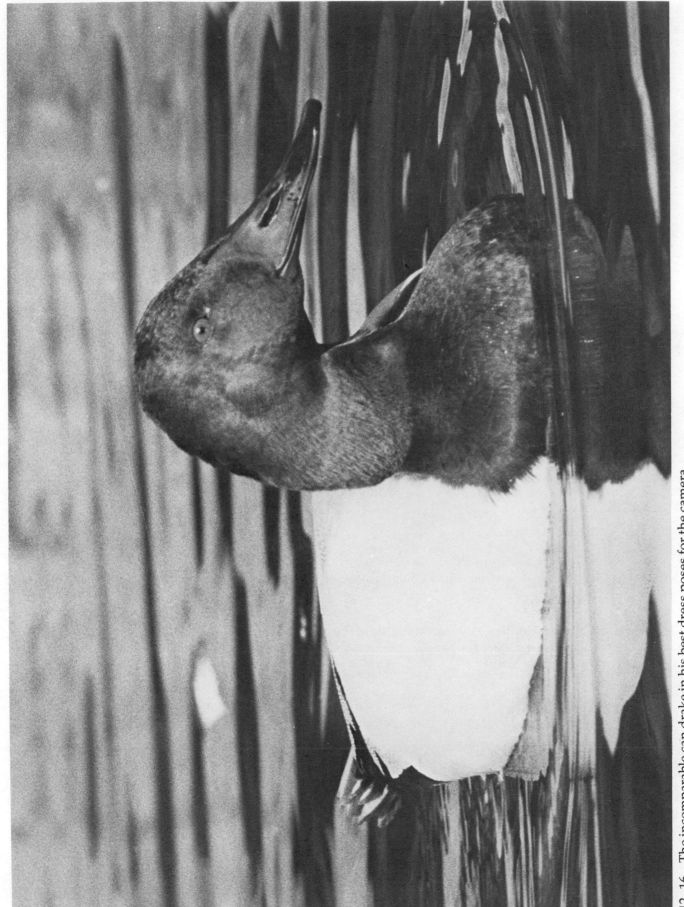

12–16 The incomparable can drake in his best dress poses for the camera.

12–17   More head positions showing different variations in the shape of the drake's heavy neck.   12–18

12–19   Another photographic study of the drake in a semialert pose.

12–20   Resting can drake. Note exposed secondary and wing covert feathers, also scapulars.

12–21   Drinking canvasback male. Especially note distinctive head shape as shown from this angle.

12–22   Male and female cans ready for instant flight.

12–23   Sleeping can drakes. Essentially the same head and neck position shown from three angles.

12–24   The female canvasback displays almost as much character as her mate. Good profile view.

12–25   The canvasback hen is a strong swimmer.

12-26   Portrait of a relaxed canvasback hen. Less colorful than her mate but in every way impressive.

12–27   Note wide body, also width of body at the inter-section of the side feathers and scapulars.

12–28   Interesting profile view of female canvasback.

12–29   Female cans have the same heavy necks of their mates.   12–30

12–31   Hen canvasback in a semialert pose.

CHAPTER   13

Scaups
Greater   *Lesser*

Greater *Aythya marila*   Lesser *Aythya affinis*

It is difficult under most conditions to accurately distinguish greater scaup from lesser scaup; therefore, these two closely related pochards will be covered in the same chapter.

As the term implies, greater scaups are usually larger and heavier than the lesser species. However, size and weight are not always positive means of identification, inasmuch as a few lesser scaups are as large or larger than some of the smaller greater scaups. The bills of the greater scaups are usually broader and heavier than the bills of their cousins but, again, in some cases these differences are small. When viewed in the sunlight, the head of the greater scaup has a pronounced green iridescence, while the slightly crested head of the lesser scaup shows purplish iridescence. Under poor lighting conditions, the head coloration of both species appears black. When identifying birds in the hand, or under certain flight conditions, there is one positive means of identification—the secondary wing feathers *only* of the lesser scaup are marked with white, whereas the greater scaup has six, or sometimes seven, inner wing primary feathers marked with white in addition to white-marked secondaries. (Color photos II-5 and 6, page 88.)

Greater scaups are found in the entire Northern Hemisphere. The ones inhabiting this continent breed in the treeless Arctic regions of Alaska and northern Canada. They winter in two widely separated areas—along the Pacific Coast from southern Alaska to California, along the coast of the middle Atlantic and

Gulf States, and the eastern Great Lakes territory. Their migration routes and habits are not clearly established. Birds banded during the winter in Oregon have been recovered in New York, while others banded in New York have been found in Washington and British Columbia. After leaving their breeding grounds in the fall, the hardy greater scaups, more maritime than the lesser species, are usually found in salt water, often far from shore, where they gather or "raft" by the thousands, and dive for small shellfish.

The widely distributed lesser scaups, or "little bluebills" as they are more often called, are an exclusive species of North America. They are more often found on inland ponds and lakes than any of the other diving ducks. Their breeding grounds extend from Alaska southeastward into the Prairie States. This species is one of the latest breeders of all the ducks—their young do not hatch until early July and ice is often starting to form on their nesting ponds before they are capable of flight. They prefer more moderate wintering climates and, although some winter as far north as Washington on the Pacific Coast and Maine on the Atlantic Coast, most of them migrate into the southern states, Mexico, Central America, and Cuba.

The eclipse plumage of the greater and lesser male scaups is similar and does not closely resemble that of the females. Their heads assume a brownish coloration but lack the white facial markings of the females. Their sides and backs become darker and are vermiculated with brown.

13–1   Although not as colorful as the canvasback and redhead, the greater scaup drake is an impressive bird. Good profile view—typical pose for diving ducks. Note leg placement.

13–2 Greater scaup male. Observe scapulars, tertials, and wing secondaries—also tail shape.

13–3 Drake is touching oil gland with bill prior to oiling and preening his feathers.

13–4 Additional profile views. Head and bill shape can be determined from these two pictorial studies. 13–5

13–6 Male and female greater scaup about to enter water.

13–7 Cross-sectional body shape and lateral leg placement can be ascertained from this front view.

13–8 Good view of the scapular and tertial feather groups—male greater scaup.

13–9   Excellent view for establishing profile of greater scaup drake on the water.

13–10   Male and female greater scaup loaf in the water.

13–11

Lesser scaup drake busily preening himself. Note slightly crested head and smaller, lighter bill.

13–12

13–13

13–14   Lesser scaup male resting but still alert.

13–15   Lesser scaup drake. Bill and body shape and location of tertials are clearly shown in this view.

13–16

Profile and front view studies of the little ''bluebill'' drake (lesser scaup).

13–17

13–18　Pictorial studies of head and body shape—lesser scaup.　13–19

More views of the lesser scaup male in different positions.

13–24
Profile and rear views of a female lesser scaup. Except for possible differences in overall size, her structural and plumage details are almost identical with the greater scaup female.
13–25

13–26 Typical profile view of a resting female greater scaup.

13–27   When used in conjunction with photo 13–28, almost all important structural details of this standing female greater scaup can be obtained.

13–28   An interesting, relaxed standing pose of a female greater scaup.

13–29   Female greater scaup preens her chest feathers.

13–30   After completing her toilet, she decides to go for a swim.

CHAPTER 14

Ring-Necked Duck

Aythya collaris

In the early days it was believed that the range of the ring-necked duck was quite small. However, this misconception was partly due to the fact that they were often incorrectly identified as scaup. Since then, ringnecks have become more readily recognized and it was found that their breeding range actually covers a large portion of central North America. During the 1930s, for some unexplained reason, a substantial number of these ducks migrated from the Great Lakes region into the extreme eastern part of Canada and Maine. From this group new settlements fanned out, until they have become fairly common in this area during the breeding season. Ringnecks winter from Vancouver to Guatemala, including all of Mexico, the Gulf States, the southeastern United States, and most of the West Indies.

The ring-necked duck seems to be more closely related to the tufted duck of Europe and Asia than other North American pochards. The name "ringnecked" is not a very descriptive one, as the very narrow, dark chestnut ring around the male's lower neck is most difficult to see when the bird is sitting on the water, and is practically impossible to see when he's in flight. The two white bands on his bill, one at the base and the other near the tip, are quite conspicuous — the name ringed-bill or ringbill would seem more definitive. The male ringneck can be distinguished from the scaups by his very white sides, black upper parts tinged with greenish iridescence, and slightly crested head. The male's white sides forward of his folded wings extend upward in sort of a hook shape — another distinguishing feature that can be seen from a considerable distance.

The female ringneck, although smaller and generally darker, can be easily confused with the female redhead. From observations made by the author, both in life and photographs, the hen ring neck appears to lack the white band at the base of the bill, so often described and illustrated as being typical of both the male and female of this species. Therefore, it appears this feature cannot always provide positive identification of the female ring-necked duck. (Color photo II-8, page 88.)

Ringnecks are ducks of the small, freshwater ponds and lakes and prefer to winter in the inland swamps and marshes. Although they spend most of their time feeding in shallow water, ringnecks can dive proficiently in deep water when necessary. They rise from the water with less effort than the other pochards and their flight is swift and direct.

The male in eclipse plumage is quite like that of the female, but the whitish markings on the face, throat, and around the eyes are lacking.

14–1   Male ring-necked duck waits patiently for his mate to finish with her primping.   14–2

14–3   Female ringneck stretches her left wing and leg.

14–4   Drake ringneck in a classic standing pose.

14–5   Male ringneck displaying.

14–6   The ringnecked drake is often mistaken for scaup; however, his sides are much whiter and he has bands on his bill. Also unlike scaup, his white sides extend up to his neck in a hooklike shape.

14–7   Good profile of a relaxed ringneck drake. Note cross-sectional body shape of female in the background.

14–8   Portrait of a sleeping hen ringneck. She lacks the white band at the base of her bill.

14–9   Studies of an alert pair of ringnecks. Crested head of male is even more noticable in this position.   14–10

14–11   Observe the distinctive shape of the drake's head.   14–12

14–13   A sleepy mated pair idle away the hours.

14–14   The chestnut-colored ring around the male's lower neck is almost always very difficult to see.

CHAPTER 15

Harlequin Duck

Histrionicus histrionicus

The vividly marked and colored harlequin ducks of the East and West Coasts are sometimes divided into two subspecies, but differences in their appearance and habits are hardly distinguishable. The large population of harlequins winter on the West Coast, and breed and nest in the mountains of the northwestern part of the continent. The much smaller number of East Coast wintering birds breed and nest on the west and southwestern coast of Greenland, the southeastern part of Baffin Island, and the northeastern coast of the Labrador Peninsula. (Color photo II-7, page 88.)

When spring is fairly well along, harlequins shift, rather than truly migrate, from the wildest and rockiest of shorelines to the high mountain lakes, where they work down the rivers and select their nesting areas where the streams have become veritable torrents. They are equally at home diving and feeding in these rushing streams as they were in the crashing, forbidding ocean surf. Superb divers and swimmers, they are capable of moving against the swift current at the bottom of the stream where they search for water insects and their larvae. The female selects a nesting spot, often under shrubs or bushes, sometimes in piles of timber or a hollow stump, but always near the rushing stream. When incubation starts, the males desert their mates and move back to the coastal areas where they wait out the flightless period during their eclipse molt.

It has been reported that newly hatched young are fed directly by the mother for a short time until they are able to find and pick up food for themselves; if this is true, the behavior of the mother duck would make her unique among all of the ducks. Unfortunately, due to their usual inaccessible nesting areas, there is much to be learned about this most interesting species. The young are introduced to falls and rapids of the mountain streams when they are very small and soon become as proficient as their mother in navigating the treacherous waters. In the early fall, as soon as the young are able to fly, the females lead the young birds to the ocean and join their mates where they can once again enjoy the wild and stormy breakers. To quote Kortright, "There is no weather too rough or habitat too wild for these truly maritime little birds."

Unlike most other diving ducks, harlequins are very much at home on land and can walk and run swiftly and gracefully with very little waddle. It has been reported that harlequins are capable of plunging into the water from the air, swimming below the surface for some distance, and bursting from under the water in full flight. The little bufflehead is believed to be the only other diver native to North America that can perform this remarkable feat.

The male harlequin in eclipse plumage is almost identical to the female.

15–1   The harlequin drake—loveliest of all the diving ducks. Unfortunately, this photo (also 15–2 and 15–3) shows the pinioned side of the bird.

The drake is fantastically marked and colored. Note thick neck.

15–4   This profile shows his primaries, broadly marked tertials, and secondaries. Note the various white spots on his plumage.

15–5   Good front view of the harlequin female. They are more at home on land than most diving ducks.

15–6   Male harlequin in a relaxed pose.

15–7   Studies of an alert drake.   15–8

15–9   Note feather detail and leg placement.

15–10   Drake in an interesting pose.

15–11   Drake preens his feathers. Note beautifully shaped, expanded tail.

15–12   Drake stretches his wing and leg.

15–13 Typical pose for female. Observe wing and scapular feather detail.

15–14 She is about to take a swim.

15–15

15–16

More studies of a mated pair.

15–17

15–18

CHAPTER 16

Hooded Merganser

Mergus cucullatus

Although not closely related, the hooded merganser has many characteristics in common with the Carolina wood duck. They both are exclusively North American species; they are about the same size; they favor wooded areas in or near the water; the females of both species nest in hollow trees whenever possible; and the males represent two of the most strikingly marked and splendidly colored of all our waterfowl. Hooded mergansers take off and fly equally as well as wood ducks and, furthermore, are very strong swimmers and possess such agility and speed under water that they are able to catch fish.

The crest of the male is magnificent and, by means of wonderful muscular feather control, can be raised and expanded or completely lowered at will. The male, especially during the mating ritual, is truly a beautiful sight. With crest fully expanded and throat area puffed out, his head appears to be almost twice its normal size and his resplendent head plumage is regally displayed. He throws back his head, then brings it to a normal position, utters a guttural call, and then makes a long rush on the water. He also rears up in the water with his bill pressed against his chest. (Color photos II-9 and 10, page 89.)

The breeding range of the hooded merganser is large and includes most of the wooded areas of the northern and eastern states and western and southern Canada. Most birds winter in fresh water, woodland swamps, and ponds of the Gulf States and east and west coastal areas.

These ducks are usually paired by the time they reach their breeding grounds, and a search for a suitable nesting site is started immediately. Female hooded mergansers and wood ducks often vie for possession of a particularly desirable nest location. When these conflicts occur, the hen wood duck is usually the victor. On occasions, however, a compromise is apparently reached and both females deposit their eggs in the same nest and, reportedly, share in the incubation process. The eggs of the hooded merganser are rather unusual, being almost spherical in shape.

The splendid hooded mergansers pictured in this book are descendants of the first ones to be bred in captivity, and were photographed at the same aviary where this occurred. This avicultural triumph was accomplished by Charles Pilling of Seattle, Washington, in 1955, when he was successful in hatching nine ducklings and rearing six. His success was the result of many years of effort. In 1950, during the hunting season, Pilling found a crippled female, and nursed her back to health. She started laying eggs during the spring of 1953, but he still had not been able to acquire a male. Late in December, 1953, he found a badly wounded male and, after caring for him constantly and force feeding him for 94 days, the bird finally regained his health and very gradually resumed normal life.

The plumage of the male in the eclipse is practically identical to the female.

16–1 The displaying hooded merganser in all his glory. His full-crested head makes him one of the most magnificent of all waterfowl.

16–2 Pair of drakes showing two variations in crest displays and head positions.

16–3 Drake in fully relaxed pose with head and crest retracted.

16–4 Striding drake about to enter the water.

16–5 Front view of the drake's amazing head and neck. Note specialized bill which is adapted for catching and holding fish.

16–6   Another study of the displaying male. He has amazing muscular control of his head feathers.

16–7   Male as viewed from the rear and front.   16–8

16–9 Pair takes a stroll. Observe the fully extended crest of the female.

16–10 A study of a talking female with crest extended.

16–11 Male in a relaxed standing pose.

16–12　Two studies showing crest feathers pulled down close to the head.　16–13

16–14　Three-quarter rear view of male showing long and strikingly marked tertials.

16–15　Female shows off her profile in the water.

16–16　Two additional studies of the male's completely variable head shape.　16–17

CHAPTER 17

Bufflehead

Bucephala albeola

The strikingly marked little bufflehead, smallest of the diving ducks, is another species found only in North America. Breeding range is primarily north of the Canadian border, and includes all but western Alaska and eastern Canada. Buffleheads winter along the entire Pacific and Atlantic Coasts as far north as the Aleutians and Nova Scotia, and generally throughout the southern half of the rest of the United States, extending into central Mexico.

The vivacious little butterballs, as they are sometimes called, seem to possess unlimited energy. They are one of a very few diving ducks who can bound from the surface (or even from under the water) in full flight. Although generally low, their flight is strong, fast, and direct. They are constantly on the move and dive at more or less regular intervals. I have never seen a bufflehead motionless, and have seen them slowly swimming in small circles even when they are asleep. They dive and swim under water equally as well as grebes, and are capable of catching small fish. Like most divers, they spend little time on land but are capable of walking fairly well.

This species was originally called "buffalo-headed" from the large size of the male's head as compared to his body. The shape of the head is extremely variable due to the fine muscular control of the long head feathers. The classic shape as shown in the accompanying drawing is seldom seen except for a short time during the prenuptial displays. At this time, the little drake is a handsome fellow with his neck extended and his beautifully shaped head puffed up to twice its nor-

mal size. Its purple, violet, and green iridescent highlights flash a veritable rainbow of colors. He is feisty and fights with the other drakes for the attention of a female. He displays to a prospective mate by standing almost erect in the water with his bill drawn down against his expanded, spotless white chest. If his advances are ignored, he dives under the female and directs his amorous attentions to another female until he finally finds his true love. (Color photo II-11, page 89.)

Buffleheads are normally tree nesters; deserted holes of woodpeckers in trees located near water are often used. Nests have been found in cavities as high as 40 feet off the ground. When trees are not available, nests are sometimes made in holes found along the banks.

In eclipse plumage, the drake is practically indistinguishable, except for his larger size, from the female.

Bufflehead drake displaying.

17–1　The handsome, sprightly, and durable bufflehead drake. He is constantly on the move.

17–2　Little drake preens his feathers. Note raised and expanded tail.

17–3 Typical profiles of drakes when on the water. 17–4

17–5 Body, head, bill, and tail shape can be determined from these two views. 17–6

17–7 Drakes expand their beautiful head feathers only during the short courtship period.

17–8 Tiny drake in an interesting pose.

17–9   Mated pair of birds pause briefly between dives.

17–10   Profile views of the little standing hen.   17–11

17–12   Two views of the small female on the water.   17–13

148   BUFFLEHEAD

17–14

17–15

17–16

17–17

Buffleheads rarely come out of the water. These were enticed with dog food.

17–18

17–19

17–20 Beautiful little male dries his wings.

17–21 Small group of buffleheads—they are excellent flyers.

17–22 A pair of butterballs flash by.

17–23 Small flock lifts easily from the water and are quickly on their way.

150

CHAPTER 18

American Common Eider

Somateria mollissima dresseri

While the common eider duck is not widely known to the people of the United States, eiderdown is a most familiar term — synonymous with great warmth and lightness. The down from the breast of an eider is probably the best and lightest (natural or man-made) heat-insulating material known. For several centuries, eiderdown has been collected on a commercial basis in Denmark, Norway, and Iceland. The eiders of these countries are completely protected and many have become semidomesticated. Usually twice during the nesting season some of the down plucked by the female eider for her nest is removed and cleaned and is used for clothing and bedding. Thirty-five to forty nests are required to produce a single pound of down. (Color photo II-12, page 89.)

During the early years the settlers and Eskimos of this continent relentlessly persecuted the eiders for their eggs, down, skins, and meat. The Migratory Bird Treaty finally gave these fine birds, actually on the verge of extinction, sufficient protection to enable them to make a comeback.

Three subspecies of the common eider are found on the North American continent: the American common eider, the Pacific comon eider (*S. m. V-nigra*), and the northern common eider (*S. m. borealis*). Except for small differences in bill development and color and head markings, these three birds are very similar. They are the largest of our ducks. The Pacific common eider often weighs well over 5 pounds; the American common eider is somewhat smaller, weighing about 1 pound less.

The American common eider breeds along the coasts of eastern Canada, Maine, and the Hudson Bay. Spring migration begins in late March or early April. According to Bent, the adult males move northward two weeks to one month ahead of female and immature birds. Nesting sites are typically located on the ground, usually less than 100 yards from salt water, and quite often in colonies. The young are led to the ocean or bay water shortly after hatching. They first find food on the surface but soon learn to dive proficiently. The ducklings tend to gather in groups, watched by only a few adult females.

Eiders are extremely hardy ducks and do not start their southward movements until late November or early December. Some of them migrate as far south as the Great Lakes inland and Massachusetts on the Atlantic Coast, while others probably move southward considerably shorter distances. During the winter months they are found in the sea, often far from the coast, moving to areas where blue mussels abound. These tasty morsels, some of them 2 inches long, are swallowed whole and in quantities and are ground to fine particles by the eiders' powerful gizzards. On occasion, the tongue of the duck is caught between the valves of the open mussel, causing death by strangulation or starvation.

18–1   The male common eider is one of our largest ducks. Note distinctive shape of his raised rearmost scapulars.

18–2   The drake's striking markings are clearly shown in this resting pose—observe head and bill shape.

18–3   His sickle-shaped tertials and unusual head markings are shown in this rear view.

18–4 Striding eider drake shows off his profile.

18–5 Body shape and lateral leg placement can be ascertained from this front view.

18–6 Hen common eider poses in a typical diving duck stance. These birds are richly colored.

18–7 Female eider displays her body shape and head profile.

18–8   Good profile of a floating hen eider.

18–9   Female eider stretches her wings.

18–10   Body shape, scapular-side feather intersection and shape of rump and tail are evident here.

CHAPTER   19

American Goldeneye

Bucephala clangula americana

American goldeneyes, commonly called whistlers (from the piercing, whistling sound made by wing primaries of mature birds during flight), are widely distributed across the continent during both their breeding and wintering seasons. At least during one time of the year, they are found in quite plentiful numbers in most of North America, except the southwestern and extreme southern part. Tree nesters, like the Barrow's goldeneyes, their breeding range follows the subarctic forest from Alaska to Newfoundland with the majority breeding north of the Canadian border. The main migration in the early fall is southward and southwestward toward the Atlantic Coast. A smaller number migrate to the Pacific Coast, from southern Alaska to Baja California. In areas where ponds or streams stay free of ice, many of this hardy species never migrate; some even winter in Yellowstone National Park where streams are warmed by hot springs.

American goldeneyes are early migrators in the spring. Starting in March, many move northward as soon as open water appears and gradually work their way to their nesting grounds as the weather becomes milder. They prefer to nest in natural cavities of trees or stumps, but will resort to other holes or openings. In their search for nesting sites, females have been known to enter cabin chimneys.

Their courtship begins as early as February and lasts through March. Probably many are mated prior to their spring migration. The prenuptial displays of these ducks are quite spectacular. The drab, eclipse dress of the drake has been completely replaced by his breeding plumage, which has reached its most beautiful stage. His puffed-up, dark head is highlighted in the sunlight with green iridescence and his bright orange feet accentuate his spotless, snow-white neck and underparts. Compared to the more somberly clad females, he is indeed a handsome fellow. One of the drakes swims about a female with his head thrust out in front near the water. Suddenly, he raises his breast and then stretches his neck and bill straight upward and calls out with a harsh, two-syllable call, *zzee-at*. He quickly snaps his head backward until his crest touches his rump or tail and then brings it forward to the normal position. At this time he lunges forward, kicking a rooster tail of water backwards and exposing his brilliantly colored feet. The female lies prone on the water when she has selected a mate and drifts in an almost lifeless manner. This pose may go on for several minutes before she alerts herself and dives with the drake following closely behind. (Color photo II-14, page 90.)

The eclipse plumage of the American goldeneye is similar to that of the Barrow's.

155

19–1

American goldeneye drakes are quite similar to the Barrow's except for shape, markings, and color of head.

19–2

Front and three-quarter rear view studies of the drake.

19–5 American goldeneye hen in a relaxed mood. Light-colored bill tip identifies her from the Barrow's hen.

19–6 Hen in classic diving duck pose.

19–7 Note low position of tail relative to water. This is typical of most diving ducks.

19–8   More studies of the female.   19–9

19–10

19–11

With his iridescent, greenish head and spotless white sides and breast, the American drake is truly an impressive bird.

19–12

CHAPTER 20

Barrow's Goldeneye

Bucephala islandica

While their range, population, and distribution are quite different, the general behavior and physical appearance of the Barrow's goldeneye and the American goldeneye are very similar. Drake Barrow's goldeneyes and American goldeneyes, however, are easily identified by quite differently shaped heads and facial markings. In the sunlight, the Barrow's dark head shows a violet iridescence while the American drake's head has a greenish iridescence. The females of the two species are almost identical but can be identified, although not easily, by small differences in bill shape and, during breeding season, by bill coloration. The female Barrow's bill is usually of an orange color and the female American has a blackish bill with orange tip. (Color photos II-15 and 16, page 90.)

The range and distribution of the Barrow's goldeneye parallels closely that of the harlequin, and they share many habits. Like the harlequin, there are two distinct populations of Barrow's goldeneyes, one on the eastern part of the continent and the other on the western part. However, unlike the harlequin, birds of these two widely separated populations are identical in every way. Also like the harlequin, Barrow's goldeneyes are not abundant in their eastern domain. The eastern birds breed in the Labrador Peninsula and western Greenland and winter along the Atlantic Coast from the St. Lawrence sometimes as far south as Long

Island. Their more abundant relatives breed and nest in the mountainous areas of the Pacific Northwest and along the Rockies as far south as central Colorado. The Barrow's wintering range is mainly on the Pacific Coast, extending south to San Francisco Bay. In early spring, they leave the coastal areas and gather in small foothill or mountain lakes—some as high as 10,000 feet in elevation—and perform their courtship rituals. With violet head feathers puffed out to their fullest extent, the drake swims up to the female of his choice with much bowing, occasionally sending a jet of water high into the air with a strong backward kick of his foot. Once mated, the males are most jealous of other would-be suitors, and there are many violent encounters, with very little physical damage. The nesting site is located near the water if possible, and is usually a natural cavity in a tree or stump, although sometimes holes made by squirrels or woodpeckers are used. Where there are no trees, nests are made in the rocks or even on the ground under bushes. Typical of most male ducks, the Barrow's goldeneye drake deserts the female as soon as the incubation period starts and returns to the sea coast.

The eclipse molt of the male is not complete. His head and neck become mottled with brown, his white face patch is barely visible, and his sides acquire brownish-gray feathers.

20–1

Mated pair of Barrow's goldeneyes preen and loaf on the shore.

20–2

20–3 Drake preens his underwing coverts under the supervision of his mate.

20–4 Profile of standing Barrow's—typical pose.

20–5 Rear view studies of a drake and hen. 20–6

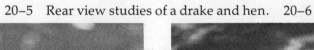

20-7 Three males and a female rest on the grass. Note female red-breasted merganser who tried to upstage them.

20-8 Drake displays his head, neck, and body shape.

20-9 Interesting head position of male.

20–10   Profile and front studies of drake's head.   20–11

20–12   Female Barrow's shows off head and body shape.

20–13   Good profile of floating drake.

20–14   Drake is faithfully followed by his newly won mate.

CHAPTER 21

Ruddy Duck

Oxyura jamaicensis jamaicensis

Although a gayly dressed and conceited playboy during his courting period, the ruddy possesses less frivolous characteristics that make him almost unique among male ducks. With the possible exceptions of the red-breasted merganser and cinnamon teal, he is the only other duck that helps protect and raise his family. Other drakes lose interest in family life almost as soon as their mates start incubating and leave to seek the easy, carefree life with fellow males. (Color photo II-13, page 90.)

His prenuptial antics provide great amusement for birdwatchers and a wide variety of poses for the wildfowl artist. He is always in motion, gliding smoothly around the female of his choice with his stiff, blackish tail feathers fanned out and held vertically, sometimes even pointed toward his black-topped, white-cheeked head puffed up by means of an air sac. He holds his head as high as his short neck will permit, then he drops his head and draws his bright blue bill tightly against his expanded chestnut-red chest. While in this position, he kicks back with both feet simultaneously, splashing water high behind him. Other times, when his bill is in the against-the-chest position, he raises his chest well out of the water and, with his tail submerged, scoots over the surface of the water. This happy lover changes instantaneously to an aggressive, determined fighter when another male recklessly shows interest in his bride-to-be.

The female ruddy duck also has characteristics unique among the ducks. She is one of the smallest of ducks, yet her eggs are enormous; they are larger than those laid by mallards and canvasbacks. According to Bent, as many as twenty eggs have been found in one nest, though the usual number is from six to ten. In order for the tiny female to cover so many eggs, they are deposited in two, sometimes three, layers. It is believed by some ornithologists that ruddys who breed in the southern parts of their range raise two broods — another characteristic that makes them unusual among the duck species.

As far as their flying, swimming, and diving abilities are concerned, ruddys more nearly resemble grebes than ducks. Also like grebes, they are seldom seen out of the water and are almost helpless on land. Capable of taking only a few steps before they fall on their breasts, they are forced to shove themselves along by pushing with their feet. Ruddys experience considerable difficulty getting off the water, and their takeoff requires gaining speed by pattering along on the surface of the water for several yards before their tiny wings are capable of sustaining flight.

Still another distinctive characteristic of the male ruddy is his molts. The ruddy acquires his breeding plumage during the spring, around March or April, and retains this plumage until about August, at which time his bright dress is replaced by the drab, grayish winter colors that resemble quite closely those of the female.

21–1 This little ruddy drake has almost acquired his breeding plumage. This photo was taken in early March.

21–2 Ruddy drake in his fall and winter plumage. He is standing in very shallow water. Observe how widely 21–3 his legs and feet are spread.

21–4

Portraits of a ruddy hen in clear water. She is one of the smallest ducks yet lays eggs as large as those of mallards and canvasbacks!

21–5

21–6   Comical little ruddy drake in one of his pre-nuptial displays. Note feather tufts on head.

21–7   Preening drake.   21–8

21–9   Drake in another courtship pose.

21–10   Drake in winter dress squats in shallow water. They leave water only infrequently and are almost helpless on land.

21–11   Two studies of the drake in breeding plumage.   21–12

PART III

GEESE AND SWANS

The best known and most admirable characteristics of geese and swans are fidelity and intelligence. These birds mate for life, and it is believed that only the widowed, or those who have been inadvertently separated, take new mates. While the male does not actually help incubate the eggs, he constantly guards the female and the nest and is prepared to give his life, if necessary, for their safety. Later, when the eggs are hatched, he does his full share in the rearing and protecting of the young. The family migrates and winters as a unit and remains together for almost a full year— until nature again arouses the reproductive urge in the parents.

During the breeding season, geese and swans are generally antisocial, and aggressively and jealously guard their own particular nesting territory — areas which vary greatly in size. They are, however, completely tolerant of ducks and other marsh birds. The nests of most geese and swans usually are piles of vegetation. Muskrat houses, located in the water, are in great demand as nesting sites. Barnacle geese and red-breasted geese prefer to nest on ledges of cliffs, and Canada geese on occasion have been known to nest in trees and on some man-made structures.

Both geese and swans have been ruthlessly slaughtered in the past and as a result have become very wary and distrusting in the wild, although they are the most easily tamed of all waterfowl. Geese and swans are considered to possess more intelligence than any other waterfowl.

In most cases, the size of the body and neck length of geese are intermediate between ducks and swans. The fore-and-aft leg position and general posture of geese, both on land and water, is quite similar to dabbling ducks. These features, plus proportionately smaller feet and longer legs, located closer together, permit geese to walk and run easily without the typical waddle of ducks. Geese, with the exception of brant and emperor geese, are more at home on land than any of the other waterfowl, and obtain most of their food by grazing like sheep and cattle on grasses and young grain sprouts. Also like grazing animals, they are very gregarious, except during the nesting season. Although geese swim well and dive adeptly when the necessity arises, most geese feed in water only occasionally. Brant are much more aquatic and feed almost exclusively on marine vegetation, except during the breeding season. Emperor geese obtain a great deal of their food along the seashore, much of which is shellfish and other marine organisms. All geese are strong flyers and for their size possess almost as much maneuverability as ducks. They can, and often do, perform spectacular aerobatics, especially when it is necessary to lose altitude rapidly. Their endurance during the long, migratory flights is legendary; they are capable of flying at great altitudes, and their flight speeds are very nearly as fast as ducks.

Swans are larger and heavier than geese — the trumpeter swan is the heaviest of all flying birds—and their necks are longer in proportion to their bodies. Because of their short legs and large feet, they walk with more effort than geese and are much more comfortable in the water than on land. They feed mainly on aquatic vegetation, which they reach with their long necks, upending like dabbling ducks when necessary. Due to their great weight, swans experience more difficulty in taking off than geese but, once in the air, they are powerful flyers. These pure white, majestic birds, with their long, outstretched necks and slow wing beat, are gracefulness personified.

The voices of geese and swans are loud and far-carrying. The large goose species and the trumpeter swan have deeper, more resonant calls as compared to the smaller geese and to whistling swans, whose voices are higher pitched. In addition to these loud calls, they all have a variety of softer, conversational calls.

Comparative bills of swans and Canada geese.

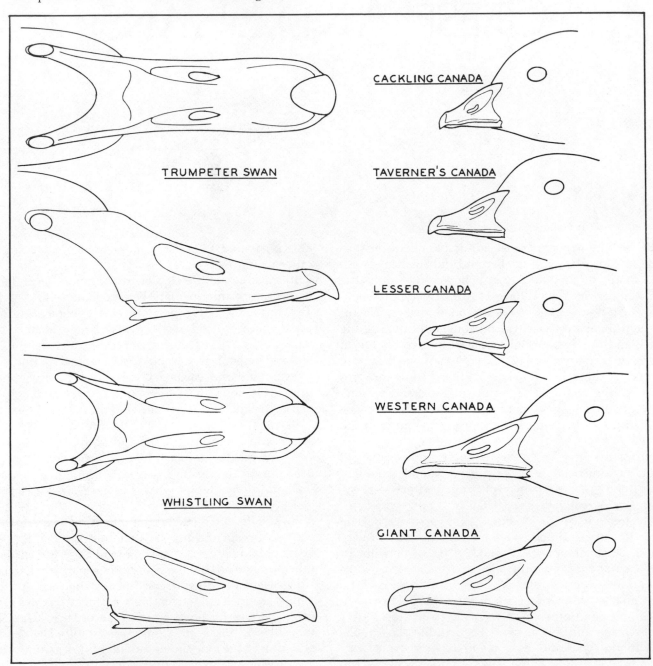

TRUMPETER SWAN

WHISTLING SWAN

CACKLING CANADA

TAVERNER'S CANADA

LESSER CANADA

WESTERN CANADA

GIANT CANADA

III–1   Western Canada goose (Chap. 22).

III–2   Pacific brant (black) (Chap. 23).

III–3   Western Canada goose.

III–4   White-fronted goose, preening (Chap. 25).

III–5   Emperor goose (Chap. 24).

III–6   White-fronted goose.

III–7　Blue goose (Chap. 26).

III–8　Snow goose, preening (Chap. 26).

III–9　Barnacle goose (Chap. 28).

III–10　　　　　　　　Blue goose.

Ross's goose (Chap. 27).　　　Snow Goose.

III–11   Red-breasted geese (Chap. 29).

III–12   Whistling swan (Chap. 30).

III–13   Trumpeter swan (Chap. 31).

CHAPTER 22

Canada Geese

Branta canadensis

The Canada goose, king of the waterfowl, is the most widely distributed and best known of all North American birds. Honkers, as birds of the larger subspecies are fondly called, are more American than the bald eagle and, in the opinion of many, should have been made our national emblem.

Many works have been written about these most remarkable birds, and they have often been eulogized in song and poetry. However, nothing does them more justice than Kortright's thumbnail character sketch: "Sagacity, wariness, strength, and fidelity are characteristics of the Canada goose, which, collectively, are possessed in the same degree by no other bird. The Canada in many respects may serve as a model for man."

The Canada goose subspecies include our largest and smallest geese; but all of these birds, regardless of size or general coloration, have in common one very conspicuous physical characteristic—a black head and neck and a white throat patch. While there is considerable intergrading among the races, eleven subspecies of the Canada goose are recognized by Delacour. The differences in overall size, coloration, length of neck, and bill size are of primary interest to the carver-artist; the feather markings of the Canada subspecies are very similar. (Color photos III-1 and 3, page 171.)

The giant Canada goose (*Branta canadensis maxima*), as the name implies, is the largest subspecies. For many years this goose was believed to have become extinct during the early 1900s. However, later reports, seldom authenticated, were made by hunters taking Canadas whose weights were in the 12- to 18-pound range. In 1960, Harold C. Hanson (*The Giant Canada Goose*) identified members of this group wintering in Minnesota. Further investigation revealed other free-flying flocks. Also, several captive groups had been perpetuated for years by Carl Strutz, Jamestown, North Dakota, and by other game breeders. The *maxima* is a large, long-necked, light-colored, relatively long-bodied bird averaging in weight from 10 to 18 pounds, with some captive birds exceeding 20 pounds. The upper part of the throat patch on many giant Canadas has a rearward hook. White on the forehead and an incomplete white ring at the base of the black neck appear to be fairly common markings. The feet and tarsi of this race are dark olive rather than black, as on other Canadas, and are larger in proportion to their bodies.

The western Canada goose (*B. c. moffitti*) is second in size to the giant Canada. A bird weighing 12 to 13 pounds is considered very large. The *moffitti* is a large, long-necked, light-colored goose. They breed and winter in the Great Plains area and the western states.

The Todd's or interior Canada goose (*B. c. interior*), the most numerous of the Canadas, is slightly smaller on the average than the western Canadas (males weigh from 6 to 11 pounds) and are quite similar in appearance, except for coloration. The color of the sides, chest, and breast of the interior Canada is intermediate between the western Canada and the dark subspecies (*B. c. occidentalis* and *fulva*). This race is found primarily in the central states.

The Atlantic Canada goose (*B. c. canadensis*) is similar in size to the interior Canada, but its coloration (sides, chest, and breast) is more nearly like that of the western Canada. These geese winter along the Atlantic Coast from Nova Scotia to the Chesapeake Bay.

There are two races of medium-to-large size, dark-colored Canada geese: the Vancouver Canada goose (*B. c. fulva*) and the dusky Canada goose (*B. c. occidentalis*). The Vancouver Canadas are of about the same weight as the western Canadas but are somewhat stockier. The coloration of their sides, chests, and breasts are the same as of their backs, scapulars, and wing coverts. The smaller dusky Canada is even darker in coloration, approaching the color of chocolate. These two subspecies breed along the British Columbia coast. The Vancouver Canadas breed and winter along the Pacific Coast from southern Alaska south to Oregon. The dusky Canadas winter mainly in the Willamette Valley of Oregon.

The small Canadas, according to Delacour, are composed of five subspecies: cackling Canada (*B. c. minima*), Richardson's Canada (*B. c. hutchinsi*), Aleutian Canada (*B. c. leucopareia*), Taverner's Canada (*B. c. taverneri*), and the lesser Canada (*B. c. parvipes*). These Canadas have shorter necks and longer wings relative to their overall body lengths as compared to the larger subspecies. Their bills are correspondingly shorter.

The cackling Canada goose is the smallest of the subspecies and is often not much larger than a mallard duck. Its coloration is dark but not quite as dark as the dusky Canada. An occasional cackler will have a narrow, incomplete white band at the base of its black neck and usually the white throat patch will be incomplete along the center line of the throat. Also, some adult cacklers have a beautiful reddish-gold tinge to their chest feathers. This subspecies has the shortest neck and the greatest wing span relative to its overall body length. In addition, cacklers have the shortest bills. They are easily distinguished from the honkers by their short necks and more rapid wing beat.

The average size of the Richardson's Canadas is slightly larger than the cacklers and they are light in coloration, similar to the Atlantic Canadas. These geese winter along the coasts of the Gulf States. Differences in size and coloration between this subspecies and the lesser and Taverner's Canadas are small. Some ornithologists believe these races should be considered a single subspecies.

The Aleutian Canada is about the same size as the Richardson's Canada. Its coloration is intermediate between the cackler and the Richardson's. A fairly wide white band at the base of the black neck appears to be a common marking on this subspecies. The population of this race is very small (possibly this subspecies is on the verge of extinction). These geese nest in the Aleutian Islands. In past years, when this subspecies was more abundant, they wintered along the coast of Washington and Oregon and in the interior valleys of California. Because of their few numbers, their present wintering range is uncertain. A number of these geese were recently banded in the Aleutians during the breeding season; several geese were later recovered in northern California.

CANADA GEESE (Branta canadensis)

Subspecies	Coloration	Wintering Area	Approximate Weight	Average Overall Length	Average Wing Span	Ratio Span to Length	Ratio Neck Length to Overall Length
LARGE (Commonly called "honkers")							
Giant Canada (B. c. maxima)	light	Northern Central States	10–18 pounds	48.0*	75.0*	156%	34–35%
Western Canada (B. c. moffitti)	light	Great Plains & Western States					
Todd's or Interior (B. c. interior)	medium	Central States & Atlantic Coast	7–13 pounds	37.2	68.8	185%	32–33%
Atlantic Canada (B. c. canadensis)	medium to light (lighter under-parts)	Atlantic Coast					
Vancouver Canada (B. c. fulva)	dark	Pacific Northwest	7–13 pounds	34.3	64.3	187%	31.5%
MEDIUM							
Dusky Canada (B. c. occidentalis)	very dark	Willamette Valley of Oregon	4–8 pounds	28.6	57.9	200%	30%
Lesser Canada (B. c. parvipes)	light	Great Plains States					
SMALL							
Taverner's Canada (B. c. taverneri)	medium to dark	California	3½–5½ pounds	26.5	52.0	196%	28–29%
Aleutian Canada (B. c. leucopareia)	medium	Washington, Oregon, and California					
Richardson's Canada (B. c. hutchinsi)	light	Texas and Mexico					
Cackling Canada (B. c. minima)	dark	So. British Columbia to California	2½–4 pounds	24.4	52.0	213%	24–25%

Note: Due to great variations in the size of individual subspecies, the above information, at best, should be considered an approximate average.

*From *The Giant Canada Goose* (Harold C. Hanson)–one specimen–

22–1   The grandest of all waterfowl—a beautiful western Canada specimen, male. The same bird is pictured on pages 179 and 180. Note the upper outline of his side feathers, also scapulars.

22–2   Another profile of the western honker.

22–3   The original "goose-step."

22–4   Goose preens his breast feathers.

22–5

More studies of this fine bird.

22–7

22–8

22–9 A tremendous amount of structural and plumage detail can be gotten from this view. Especially note leg placement, cross-sectional body shape, position of crossed primaries, and overlapping of tertials and scapulars.

22–10   Western Canada goose poses with one wing partially expanded.   22–11

22–12   22–13

He meticulously attends to his grooming.

22–14   22–15

Head, neck, and bill studies of a western Canada goose.

22–20

Some studies of the honker's many flight positions.

22–21

22–22

22–23

22–24 The western Canada goose's beautifully marked scapulars, side feathers, and wing secondaries and coverts are clearly shown here.

22–25 Detail study of his large tertials, position of crossed primaries, and secondaries. Also note tail position.

22–26 Rear view of Canada goose on the water clearly shows body shape and feather detail.

22–27 The large honker rides buoyantly on the water—good pose.

22–28

Profile studies of an Atlantic Canada gander. Observe his heavy neck. He is usually slightly darker in coloration than the western Canada.

22–29

22–30

Same gander shown on page 187, but this time he is with his mate.

22–31

22–32

The large Vancouver Canada goose—he is quite dark in coloration.

22–33

22–34

The smaller dusky Canada goose is even darker than the Vancouver Canada. His color approaches chocolate.

22–35

22–36   He ruffles his feathers and assumes a threatening pose.

22–37   Good head, neck, and bill studies of the dusky.

22–38   Lesser Canada gander. He is quite light in coloration. They vary greatly in size.

22–39   Same male shown with his mate.

22–40   Cackling Canada goose in feeding pose. He is quite small and dark. Note small bill.

22–41   Same bird shown from the front.

22–42   Little cackler in a classic pose. He held this exact position for about five minutes.

22–43 Front view of a cackler. Note throat patch. It is often discontinuous on bottom of throat.

22–44 Little cackler takes a walk in the rain.

22–45 Two more studies of the tiny Canada goose. 22–46

22–47 Alert cackling Canada goose.

22–48 Cackler shows another head position.

22–49

22–50

Three studies of a Taverner's Canada goose.

22–51

CHAPTER 23

Brant= Pacific and Atlantic

Pacific *Branta bernicla orientalis*　　　　Atlantic *Branta bernicla hrota*

Two brant species are indigenous to North America: Pacific or black brant of the Pacific Coast and Atlantic or American brant of the Atlantic Coast. These plump, short-necked, long-winged birds, slightly larger than a mallard duck, are true sea geese. Except during their nesting season, they are seldom away from the coastal waters. Well-developed salt glands enable them to subsist entirely on salt water and coastal vegetation.

Brant are graceful little geese. They sit buoyantly on the water with tails — almost completely covered by snow-white coverts — held high. Their well-shaped heads and small bills move daintily on smoothly flowing necks. The flight of the brant is swift, strong, and unusually low — just above the waves. Their flight formation differs, too, from that of other geese, as they typically fly in long, undulating lines formed at right angles to the direction of flight. (Color photo III-2, page 171.)

Although difficult to distinguish in flight, the two species have some differences in coloration and markings. The chest, neck, and breast of the black brant is dullish black; the coloration of the American brant in these areas is slightly grayer. The black brant has a chokerlike collar approximately 1 inch wide and incomplete at the back of the neck; the throat collar on the American brant is incomplete at both the front and back of the neck. The black chest of the black brant blends into the breast with no pronounced demarcation and shades into lighter and lighter slaty-brown,

finally merging into the white underside about 5 inches forward of the tail. The black chest of the American brant is sharply defined against the light-gray breast that blends into the white underside approximately 7 inches from the tail. The American brant's side feathers are considerably lighter in coloration than the black brant's.

The back feathers, scapulars, and most wing coverts on juveniles of both species are edged with buffy-white. The throat collars of juveniles may be indistinct or missing.

The black brant breeds along the Arctic coast of Alaska and Canada, the islands to the north, and on the Arctic tundra of northwestern Siberia, east to the Khatanga River. The wintering population on this continent is distributed from southern British Columbia to Baja California. The American brant breed even farther north in eastern Arctic Canada, the islands to the north, northern Greenland, and Spitsbergen. The wintering population in North America is found along the Atlantic Coast from New Jersey to North Carolina. There may be some overlapping of nesting grounds but, apparently, very little crossbreeding occurs between these two brant species, although a few specimens of intermediate colorations have been recorded. The small amount of crossbreeding can probably be accounted for by the fact that most, if not all, breeding brant are mated prior to reaching the nesting area.

23–1   The black, or Pacific brant, is a beautiful and graceful little sea goose, not much larger than a mallard duck.

23–2

Black brant in threatening poses. Note smooth-flowing lines of neck and body.

23–3

23–4   Front view showing body contours and legs.

23–5   Three-quarter rear view. Observe how his tail is almost covered with the white coverts.

23–6   Brant in a feeding pose. Note how the feathers smoothly cover his right leg.

23–7   Black brant drinking. The graceful lines of his neck are most obvious.

23–8   Little brant forages on the shore.

23–9   Rear view. Note body shape and leg placement.

23–10   Profile studies of the black brant.   23–11

23–12   Interesting pose—note head and bill shape.

23–13   Brant in another feeding pose.

23–14

23–15

Details of black brant's chokerlike collar.

23–17

23–16 Good front view showing cross-sectional shape of body.

23–18 His smooth profile contours are displayed here.

23–19 Good standing pose.

23–20   Three black brant swim toward the camera.

23–21   Four rear view studies on floating black brant.

23–22   Brant are one of the most graceful of all waterfowl when on the water.

202   PACIFIC AND ATLANTIC BRANT

23–23   Group of black brant. They usually fly in wide, undulating lines.

23–24   Brant are strong flyers. They fly low, often just above the waves.

23–25   Five different flight positions.

23–26   The Atlantic, or American, brant is identical structurally to the black brant, but has lighter sides and breast. In addition, his chokerlike collar is smaller and discontinuous on both the front and back of his neck.

Two studies of the Atlantic brant in a resting pose.

23–29 Atlantic brant striding with head in an alert position.

23–30 Brant in a pleasing pose.

23–31 American brant cropping grass.

23–32 Rear view of a striding American brant.

23–33 Brant float lightly and move daintily on the water. 23–34

CHAPTER 24

The Emperor Goose

Anser canagicus

Bent describes the emperor goose as the "handsomest and least known of American geese." Van Campen Hellner (*Duck Hunting*) states they are the "wariest of waterfowl." Whether they are the handsomest and wariest of geese may be argued by many; but, without doubt, due to their very limited range, they are seen by fewer hunters and bird watchers than any other goose species in North America.

In some respects, the emperor goose resembles the blue goose; however, the dark, brownish-black underneck and orange-yellow tarsi and feet of the emperor are prominent features which help reduce possible confusion in identification. Also, because of the wide separation of their ranges, there is very little likelihood of these two species being seen together. (Color photo III-5, page 172.)

Emperor geese breed along the almost inaccessible coastal marshes of western Alaska in the Seward Peninsula and Morton Sound areas. Some breed along the eastern coast of Siberia at about the same latitudes. They are already mated when they arrive at their breeding grounds during the last part of May. During this period, the males are very jealous and strongly resent any approaches made toward their mates. Nesting sites are usually selected in the driftwood debris that marks the high tide line along the coasts, although some nests are located 10 miles or so inland. The young are hatched in late June or early July. About two or three weeks after the young appear, the adult birds molt and become flightless. During this period, both young and old are very vulnerable to depredation by their natural enemies and, at least in the past, by natives who captured some of these very helpless birds for food. By early August, the adults have again acquired their flight feathers and are able to fly, as are the young birds.

Emperor geese are almost as much at home in the ocean and on the coast as black brant. Unlike the plant-loving brant, their food during the winter consists mainly of mussels and shellfish. In the spring, they forage on grasses and berries like other geese. As previously mentioned, Eskimos take some birds, also their eggs, for food during the nesting season. However, these geese remain at all times far from most humans. The population of emperor geese is estimated at approximately 200,000, and their survival is not threatened. An occasional straggler (probably separated from his group by strong, northwest gales) is seen as far south as California. In the winter of 1970, a large number of bird watchers were delighted to spot three emperor geese on a tidal flat near Huntington Beach, California.

24–1 The beautifully marked and colored emperor goose. Because of his extreme northern range, he is rarely seen in the contiguous United States.

24–2 Emperor goose in a typical feeding position. Note the complicated markings of his body feathers.

24–3 This goose is fluffing his scapulars. Also note how the upper side feathers stand out against his wing.

24–4 Mated pair take a walk. The bird in the foreground is the female. Typical of all geese, she has the same markings and coloration of her mate.

24–5 Much structural and plumage detail can be ascertained from this rear view.

24–6 In taking a step, the right foot is pointed inward and moved under the center of the body while the left foot is brought forward.

24–7

24–8

Additional photographic studies of the emperor goose.

24–9

24–10

24–11   Emperors are hardy sea geese and spend most of their time in the salt water of the Far North.   24–12

CHAPTER 25

White=Fronted Goose

Anser albifrons frontalis

Although rarely found east of the Mississippi River, the beautiful white-fronted geese are fairly abundant winter residents in California, along the coasts of Texas and Louisiana, and in parts of Mexico. During migration, whitefronts make many stops in Alberta, Manitoba, and the Great Plains states of the Central Flyway and parts of Washington and Oregon in the Pacific Flyway. They breed in the Arctic tundra of Alaska, from the Bering Sea eastward to central Arctic Canada, and in northeastern Siberia.

"Specklebelly" or "speck," as the white-fronted goose is commonly called, is a medium-size goose — males have an average weight of about 5½ pounds, an average wing span of 63 inches, and an average overall length of 29 inches. The adult goose is strikingly marked with a pink bill shading into pale blue at the base, a white band around the front of the face at the base of the bill, yellow to yellow-orange feet, and variable black and white markings on the breast. Immature birds (most whitefronts do not mature until their second, sometimes third year) lack the white facial band and the black and white breast markings, and their feet and bills are duller in color. (Color photos III-4 and 6, page 172.)

Whitefronts are the only geese on this continent whose heads (except for the white face), necks, chests, and upper parts are solidly brown. Due to this color characteristic, they are normally easy to identify when on the water. The yellow feet and variable black and white breast markings make the adults quite conspicuous in flight; and even the immature whitefronts are easy to identify when flying at close range. At greater distances, however, whitefronts are much more difficult to identify, as they tend to resemble Canada geese in color. This is because aerial perspective causes the brown to appear gray. Also, the V-shape flight formation of the white-fronted geese is similar to that of the Canadas. Groups of whitefronts are often seen flying with flocks of snow geese or the small-to-medium-size Canadas.

Another species of the white-fronted goose, the tule goose (*Anser albifrons gambelli*) has wintered, at least in the past, in the Sacramento Valley of California. The tule goose is larger, heavier (weights up to 10 pounds have been recorded), and has similar markings to those of the white-fronted goose, but is somewhat darker in coloration. Its neck is longer in proportion to its body than the whitefront, and its bill is considerably longer (approximately 40 percent) and heavier. There is concern that this species is on the verge of extinction; it may, in fact, already be extinct.

25–1   The strikingly marked white-fronted goose. He is rarely seen east of the Mississippi River.

25–2

Whitefronts grazing on new grass shoots. Like Canadas, one goose is usually on the alert.

25–3

Studies of adult specklebellies. They do not acquire their white faces and black breast markings until the second or third year.

25-8 Preening whitefronts. Geese, like all waterfowl, spend a great deal of time each day caring for their   25-9
plumage.

25-10 Note white on throat at base of bill. This is typical of all adult whitefronts.

25-11 Well-fed whitefront in a relaxed mood.

216   WHITE-FRONTED GOOSE

25–12   Observe individual feather detail of scapulars. The ridges and furrows of the neck feathers on these geese are more irregular than those of snow geese.

25–13   Good profile of floating white-fronted goose. Note definite intersection line between side feathers and scapulars. Note background bird stretching for food.

25–14

25–15

25–16

25–17

More studies of preening whitefronts.

25–18

25–19

25–20   Note shape and markings of large tertial feathers.   25–21

Four different feeding positions. Whitefronts obtain almost all of their food on land.

25–24
25–25

CHAPTER 26

Snow and Blue Geese

Anser coerulescens coerulescens

Lesser snow geese and blue geese are identical except for coloration. Most ornithologists now believe they are color phases of the same species. A smaller group still maintains the birds are two distinct subspecies and the intergrading between them is a result of hybridism, as snow and blue geese readily interbreed. Regardless of whether they are separate subspecies or color phases, these geese are colorful birds and make most interesting subjects for the artist. (Color photos III-7, 8, and 10, page 173.)

Snow and blue geese are the most abundant geese in North America. Although they winter in several concentrated areas — the Sacramento, San Joaquin, and Imperial Valleys of California (white phase only); along the southeast coast of Texas (white phase predominant); and the Louisiana coast (blue phase predominant) —they are seen during migration along all of the flyways. White phase snow geese breed in Arctic Siberia, the Arctic coast of Alaska, and the Arctic islands east to the Baffin Islands. The blue phase birds nest in the Baffin and Southampton Islands.

These geese, when migrating or flying to feeding areas, maintain long, diagonal lines or V-shaped formations. Their constant talking can be heard for considerable distances.

As recently as 50 or 60 years ago, the blue phase goose was relatively rare. Now, there are more blues in the Mississippi Flyway than white birds and they are increasing at a rate of about 2 percent per year. Although there have been a few specimens taken, the blue phase is a rarity along the Pacific Flyway. It is very possible we are witnessing evolution — survival of the fittest — between these two color phases. F. G. Cooch (*Waterfowl Tomorrow*) reports blue geese have a higher rate of survival at the nesting grounds, possibly because they nest later than white phase geese and their nests are less likely to be subject to flooding during the incubation period. Also, by then the predators have had an opportunity to satiate their appetites somewhat at the expense of the earlier white birds. Cooch further states that the survival rate of the blue phase birds is higher during hunting season as hunters seem to favor the big white birds. According to John Lynch, U.S. Fish and Wildlife biologist, blue phase birds predominate in family groups of mixed color by a ratio of 1.78 to 1. In families where the parents were a blue goose and a snow goose, the ratio of young blues to young whites was 2.46 to 1. Another important factor contributing to the increase in blue phase geese is that male snow geese are reluctant to mate with female blue geese, while female snows readily breed with male blues. All of these factors point to an eventual takeover of the white phase by the blue phase in the Central and Mississippi Flyways. There appears to be little likelihood of blue geese becoming predominant in the Pacific Flyway in the foreseeable future.

26-1   A mixed group   three blue geese, two snow geese, and a little Ross's gander behind the snows. Snow goose on right is taking a step—note foot placement.

26–2   Two blues and a snow walk in the rain—a study of profiles.

26–3   Two relaxed snow geese. Note position of right foot and shape of side feather group on the standing goose.

26–4   Good profile of a snow goose in feeding position.

26–5   Snow goose with partially extended left wing. Attention is called to the long tertial and greater covert feathers.

26–6   Mated pair of snows. Cross-sectional body shape and leg placement are evident.

26–7 Note flowing lines of chest and neck—also shape of head.

26–8 Front view of snow goose showing head, neck, body, and leg shape.

26–9 Studies of different head positions.

26–10 Two very much alert snow geese. Note crossed primaries and shape of back.

26–11   26–12   26–13

26–14   26–15

Detail head and bill studies. Note how neck feathers lie in ridges and furrows.

26–16   The heads of these geese are often stained from the iron in the water.

26–17 Striding blue goose. Observe legs and contours of under parts.

26–18 Blue goose relaxes wings as he rests.

26–19

26–20

Front, rear, and profile views of blue geese.

26–21

26–22

26–23

Profile studies of floating snow geese.

26–24

26–25

26–26 Especially observe crossed primaries, tertials, and greater covert feather groups. Also note intersection of side feathers with scapulars and wing.

26–27

Profile studies of a floating blue goose. Note large tertials and greater covert feathers. The scapulars show quite prominently.

26–28

26–29 A lone blue goose flies with snow geese—a rare sight on the West Coast. Photos below show snow geese in a few of their flight positions.

26–30

26–31

26–32

26–33

230

CHAPTER 27

Ross's Goose

Anser rossi

The lovely, little Ross's goose, the rarest and one of the smallest of North American geese, is seldom seen except in California and only during the winter. Although scientifically described and named in 1861 by John Cassin after Bernard Rogan Ross, Chief Factor of the Hudson's Bay Company, little was known of the Ross's goose except its wintering habits. In 1938 or 1940 (there appear to be two different accounts), Angus Gavin of the Hudson's Bay Company at last found its breeding grounds near the Perry River, almost 50 miles north of the Arctic Circle. In 1949, this area was again visited by Hanson, Gueneau, and Scott who reported there were no Ross's geese nesting on the lakes where they were previously found by Gavin (Delacour). From the number of nests found in the general area, it was determined by these three that the world population of Ross's geese may have been less than 2,000. However, in 1960, Thomas W. Barry (*Waterfowl Tomorrow*) surveyed a larger area and counted at least 9,000 Ross's geese, most of which were nesting approximately 100 miles east of the Perry River. Snow geese were also nesting in this area and, because of the difficulty in making positive identification between these two species, Barry reports that considerably more of these little geese could have been nesting there. Other nesting areas have been found in the Southampton Island area (northwest part of Hudson Bay). It is Barry's belief that Ross's geese may also be found nesting with snow geese along the south central shores of Baffin Island.

The Ross's goose is classified as one of the group of threatened species — its present population is somewhat more than 30,000. This bird, except for having a shorter bill in proportion to its head, appears to be a miniature snow goose and is commonly mistaken for one. Because of difficulty in identification, hunters are now allowed a bag limit of one bird a day in the Central and Pacific Flyways. The Ross's goose has at least two characteristics which make identification at a distance possible — they are considerably less talkative when flying than snow geese and their flight is much more erratic. These little geese often dart from side to side and change altitude slightly — their black-tipped, white wings flash in the sunlight as they bank rapidly, first one way and then the other. Also, they often fly in disorganized groups compared to the long, diagonal lines of snow geese. I have seen large groups — probably several hundred birds — of Ross's geese on a number of occasions that were easily identifiable over a distance of several miles by their flight mannerisms, flashing wings, and tight grouping. They often intermingle with snow geese and are then somewhat easier to identify by comparison in size. (Color photo III-10, page 173.)

Immature Ross's geese, like immature snow geese, are much grayer on their upper parts than their pure-white parents; their feet and bills are also paler in color. According to Bent, immature birds acquire their adult plumage when they are about 10 months old.

27–1   A pair of Ross's geese. They are miniature snow geese except that their bills are relatively smaller as compared to their heads, and their necks are shorter and heavier.

27–2   A lovely little Ross's in a feeding position. Note leg positions and flowing chest-neck lines.

27-3   A group of Ross's geese. A great deal of structural information can be obtained from these views.

27-4   Relaxed little Ross's goose. The black feather showing on the left side is apparently an inner primary that was not pinioned.

27–5   Two studies of a large Ross's gander and a small female snow goose.   27–6

27–7   Rare photo of Ross's geese in flight.

27–8   Studies of alert Ross's geese.

CHAPTER   28

Barnacle Goose

Branta leucopsis

Barnacle geese, although natives of Europe, are fairly frequent visitors to eastern North America. They breed along the northeastern coast of Greenland and on the Spitsbergen Islands north of Norway. Their wintering range includes most of the extreme northwestern part of Europe, but on occasion they are seen inland as far south as Switzerland and Austria. Barnacle geese are very common winter residents of the west coast of Scotland and depart this area in large numbers for their breeding grounds. (Color photo III-9, page 173.)

When arriving at their nesting areas, most mated pairs select nesting sites high up on ledges of precipitous cliffs and, in some cases, atop pinnacles of rock. Inasmuch as there is little or no feed or water at these nesting locations, the newly hatched goslings must somehow reach the valley floors in order to survive.

There has been conjecture as to whether the parents carry the young down or if the downy puffballs make the almost vertical descent, sometimes several hundred feet, by floating down, the speed of the fall being possibly lessened by strong air currents flowing up the face of the cliffs. According to Salomonsen (*The Birds of Greenland*), both means of making the descent have been witnessed. An adult male, and also female barnacle geese have been seen carrying goslings down, one at

a time, in their bills. In another instance, a gosling was carried on the back of one of the parents. They have also been observed floating down unaided from heights of 100 feet and landing safely in the water. Other families, where the terrain permitted, were seen walking down to a lake. After spending one to two weeks on the inland ponds and lakes, the young are led to the coast where they are joined by numbers of other families.

Although barnacle geese somewhat resemble brant, feed on tidal mud flats and in the shallow, offshore waters on occasion, and are seldom found far from the coast, they are as much land geese as brant are sea geese. Their favorite food is the short, sweet grass found in the coastal areas fed by fresh water.

The breeding grounds of the barnacle goose in northeastern Greenland is fairly close, or may even possibly overlap, the breeding grounds of the Atlantic, or American, brant. It is possible a few barnacle geese may somehow get separated from their own kind and migrate to the eastern seaboard of North America with the brant. Another possibility, of course, is that these occasional visitors are carried inadvertently far south and west of their normal migration routes by strong winds during violent storms.

28–1   The distinctively marked barnacle geese are natives of Europe; however, stragglers quite often visit the East Coast.

28–2   Barnacle geese are a little larger than brant.

236   BARNACLE GOOSE

28–3   Mated pair. Gander on left stretches his long neck for a better view.

28–4   An interesting pose of a pinioned bird. Note tail shape and position of left foot.

28–5   Barnacle goose in feeding position.

28–6   The small barnacle goose looks into the camera. Note head, neck, and body contours.   28–7

28–8   Profile of a swimming barnacle goose.

CHAPTER 29

Red-Breasted Goose

Branta ruficollis

Unfortunately for us, this most colorful and lovely little goose is an extremely rare visitor to western North America. However, it is now being more commonly sought after and propagated by aviculturalists and can be seen quite often in parks, zoos, and in private collections. The red-breasted goose, sometimes called the Siberian goose, is the most beautiful of all the geese, which is the reason it has been included in these pictorial studies of North American waterfowl. (Color photo III-11, page 174.)

They breed in northern Siberia, generally between the Ob and the Khatanga Rivers and in their deltas. Their wintering grounds are around the southern shores of the Caspian and Aral Seas, where they feed on crops and grasses like other geese, but move back to the salt water at night and spend their resting period on sand bars or islands. Red-breasted geese are often seen in the company of lesser white-fronted geese. Northward migration starts in February and March and they reach their breeding grounds in early June. These little geese have somewhat similar nesting habits to those of barnacle geese, preferring holes in cliffs and banks that are protected by brush or shrubs.

Redbreasts are graceful and dainty little birds—very nearly the size of cackling Canada geese. Their necks are probably about the same length as the cacklers but, because of manelike feathers on the hind neck and nape, they appear to be considerably thicker. Also like the cackler, their wing span is about twice their overall body length. Johnsgard (*Waterfowl*) lists the red-breasted's overall length as 21–22 inches. According to Delacour, his bill size and length of tarsi are about 15 percent smaller than those of the cackler.

This little goose is exquisitely marked and colored—a beautiful study of contrasts. His bright, chestnut-red chest, neck front and sides, and cheeks are demarcated from his rich, black head, hind neck, upper body parts, sides, and breast with white stripes. The upper side feathers are heavily edged with white. His black tail is strikingly offset by snow white coverts, flanks, and belly. His large wings are of the same deep, shiny black with the greater and a few middle coverts edged with white.

Delacour writes: "Their voice is high-pitched, pleasant and rather musical, if a little harsh, their calls consisting of a two-syllabled staccato 'Kee-kwa,' 'Kik-wit,' 'ti-che' and so forth, the second note a little broken. They hiss frequently and squeak constantly in an irritated way while feeding."

Red-breasted geese adapt extremely well to captivity — even those that are captured in the wild become tame in a short time. They are a lovely addition to any collection of waterfowl.

29–1

The red-breasted goose's striking markings are quite apparent in these two views. Note manelike feathers on back of neck. In size, he is almost identical to the cackling Canada.

29–2

29–3   These front and rear views provide a great deal of structural and plumage detail.   29–4

29–5   Two interesting views of the world's most beautiful and graceful goose.

29–6 Good profile of the graceful little red-breasted on the water.

29–7 The little red-breasted goose floats buoyantly on the water. Observe his prominent scapulars. 29–8

29–9 Studies showing head, neck, and bill detail. Bill of red-breasted is very similar to cackling Canada. 29–10

CHAPTER 30

Whistling Swan

Cygnus columbianus columbianus

The elegant whistling swan, one of our two native swan species, while substantially reduced in numbers from earlier years, is still fairly common during the winter in areas on both the East and West Coasts. Whistlers nest in the most remote regions of Arctic Alaska and Canada, places that are not likely ever to be disturbed by man to any great extent. These very wary birds have been protected since 1916; therefore, it is unlikely their present numbers will ever again be greatly diminished.

Although considerably smaller, whistling swans are not always easily distinguished from trumpeter swans. Most whistling swans have a yellow patch on their bills, just forward of each eye, but, unfortunately, some do not. In flight, the two species can be identified by their voices. The call of the whistling swan is high-pitched as compared to the trumpeter's low, extremely resonant, hornlike call. Whistlers can be distinguished from snow geese by their longer necks, slower wing beat, and completely white wings. (Color photo III-12, page 174.)

Whistling swans in flight are the ultimate in gracefulness. They migrate in small V-shaped flocks, led by a strong mature male, or cob, as he is called. The young birds, or cygnets, normally fly farther back in the formation where less effort is required to maintain the speed of the group. When traveling to their feeding grounds, they fly in long, curving lines, or sometimes in irregular formation.

Whistling swans do not reach full maturity until they are five or six years old but occasionally mate when they are only three years of age. Like geese, they mate for life, but if one is killed, the other may take a new mate. Nests are usually made on a mound of moss or dried grass, often near the water but sometimes as far as a half mile from the shoreline. Sometimes, the female will lay as many as seven eggs, though four is the average number. The beautiful, downy young hatch in 32 to 35 days. Approximately two weeks after the cygnets are hatched, the female molts and becomes flightless. About the time she is able to fly, the cob molts his flight feathers, so, normally, one of the parents is capable of flight at all times. The cygnets are flying in about 2½ months, and are ready to migrate when they are 3½ months old. Usually only two or three of the young survive; they remain constantly with their parents for the first year.

30–1 Mated pair of whistling swans in semialert and sleeping poses. Note serpentine convolutions of sleeping bird's neck.

30–2 Whistler in a very graceful drinking or feeding pose. Useful view for establishing profile tarsi location and body and chest shape.

30–3 Excellent profile view and front view of striding whistling swan. Note wide placement of powerful legs 30–4 and cross-sectional body shape.

30–5 The whistler's long neck is very flexible and is always held in graceful, flowing lines.

30–6 The whistler in another interesting pose.

30-7

Resting poses showing relaxed and alert head and neck positions. Observe position of his large feet.

30-8

30–9   These rear views are useful in establishing body cross-sectional shape of the floating bird.   30–10

30–11   The elegant and graceful whistling swan displays his classic profile.

CHAPTER   31

Trumpeter Swan

Cygnus cygnus buccinator

By 1900, trumpeter swans, the most majestic of our waterfowl and also the heaviest of all flying birds, were on the verge of extinction. During the eighteenth and nineteenth centuries, both the trumpeter and whistling swans were ruthlessly hunted. Their skins were used for powder puffs and the quills for pens. The Hudson's Bay Company reportedly sold over 100,000 swan skins to the London market between 1823 and 1880. Very probably a large percentage of these were trumpeter swan skins, inasmuch as this species nested in areas, both in the United States and Canada, where the fur trade flourished. (Color photo III-13, page 174.)

Trumpeter swans, in former years, bred throughout the northern, western, and central parts of North America, from Alaska and northern Canada as far south as Missouri. Many of them wintered in the central Atlantic States, along the Ohio and Mississippi River regions, in the Gulf States, and in northwestern Oregon. They now avoid the long, dangerous flights and migrate, or more correctly, move only far enough to find open water and food. Their formerly wide range has now been reduced to a few scattered colonies in southern Alaska, British Columbia, Alberta, Montana, Wyoming, and South Dakota.

Although swans have been protected since 1918 by the Migratory Bird Treaty Act with Great Britain (including Canada), the number of trumpeters inhabiting the United States in 1931 was believed to have been only thirty-five. In recent years, strong comebacks have been made by this species at the Red Rock Lakes National Wildlife Refuge in southwestern Montana and in the Yellowstone Park area. Unlike other waterfowl that, for the most part, are very gregarious, trumpeter swans are very antisocial during the breeding season. They apparently return to the same nest every year; when these sites have been selected on a small lake or slough, the breeding pair will not permit other swans to trespass. Nests on larger bodies of water are usually located ½ mile apart and territorial rights are rigidly enforced. Breeding trumpeters do not object to ducks and swamp birds nesting within a few feet of them, but will not permit the intrusion of other swans or geese. As a result of their large breeding area requirements, established colonies soon become saturated. Flocks of nonbreeding birds, many already mated, have difficulty not only finding nesting sites but also feeding areas. Although attempts have been made to relocate some of these nonbreeding pairs to other locations, these efforts have been only partially successful.

According to Delacour, "Trumpeter swans do very well in captivity. They soon become tame, prove completely hardy, easy to feed, and they breed readily." They do, however, retain much of their inability to get along with other large birds.

While the extinction of the trumpeter swan is no longer threatened, their distribution and numbers will very likely always remain limited.

31–1　The majestic trumpeter swan is the heaviest of all flying birds.

31–2　Except for overall size and weight and minor differences in bill shape, trumpeters are like whistlers.

31–3

31–4

Studies of the proud trumpeter from the front. They sometimes attain weights of 35 pounds, overall length of 72 inches, and a wing span of 98 inches.

31–5

31–6   Head and bill details can be obtained from these two views. Also see drawing on page 170.   31–7

31–8   31–9

In flight, swans are gracefulness personified.

31–10

APPENDIX: Bibliography, Topography of Waterfowl, Skeletal Structure of Wings and Legs

Waterfowl Pictures and Life Histories

Allan, Arthur A. *Stalking Birds with Color Camera*. National Geographic Society, Washington, D.C. (out of print).

———. *Duck Hunting with Color Camera*. National Geographic, October 1951.

Audubon. National Audubon Society, 1130 Fifth Avenue, New York, N.Y. 10028.

Bauer, Erwin A. *Duck Hunter's Bible*. Paperback, Doubleday, Garden City, N.Y.

Bent, Arthur Cleveland. *Life Histories of North American Waterfowl* (two volumes). Dover Publications, New York.

Butcher, Devereau. *Seeing America's Wildlife in our National Refuges*. Devin-Adair, New York (out of print).

Delacour, Jean. *The Waterfowl of the World*. Dover Books, New York.

Einarsen, A. S. *Black Brant: Sea Goose of the Pacific*. University of Washington Press.

Hanson, Harold C. *The Giant Canada Goose*. Southern Illinois University Press.

Hochbaum H. A. *The Canvasback on a Prairie Marsh*. Stackpole Co., Harrisburg, Pa.

Johnsgard, Paul A. *Waterfowl*. University of Nebraska Press.

———. *Handbook of Waterfowl Behavior*. Cornell University Press.

———. *Waterfowl of North America*. Indiana University Press.

Kortright, Francis H. *The Ducks, Geese, and Swans of North America*. Stackpole Co., Harrisburg, Pa.

Lansdowne, J. Fenwick, and Livingston, John A. *Birds of the Eastern Forest* (two volumes). Houghton Mifflin, Boston, Mass.

———. *Birds of the Northern Forest*. Houghton Mifflin, Boston, Mass.

Linduska, Joseph P., ed. *Waterfowl Tomorrow*. U.S. Government Printing Office, Washington, D.C.

———. *National Wildlife*. 1412 Sixteenth St., N.W., Washington, D.C. 20036.

Queeny, Edgar M. *Prairie Wings*. Lippincott, Philadelphia and New York (out of print).

Rand, Austin L. *American Water and Game Birds*. Dutton, New York (out of print).

Sprunt, Alexander, and Zim, Herbert. *Game Birds*. Western, New York.

Van Wormer, Joe. *The World of the Canada Goose*. Lippincott, Philadelphia and New York.

———. *Water, Prey, and Game Birds of North America*. National Geographic Society, Washington, D.C.

Williams, Cecil S. *Honker*. D. Van Nostrand Co., Princeton, N.J.

Bird Anatomy

Aymar, Gordon. *Bird Flight*. Dodd, Mead, New York (out of print).

Beebe, C. William. *The Bird*. Dover, New York (out of print).

Darling, Lois and Louis. *Bird*. Houghton Mifflin, Boston (out of print).

Pettingell, Olin Sewall, Jr. *Ornithology*. Burgess, Minneapolis, Minn.

Bird Anatomy for Artists, Structural Dimensions, and Bill and Foot Photographs

Burk, Bruce. *Game Bird Carving*. Winchester Press, New York.

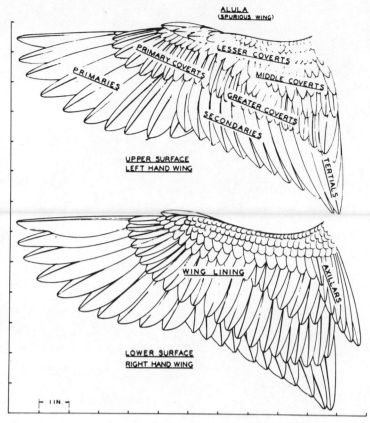

Wing of a cinnamon teal.

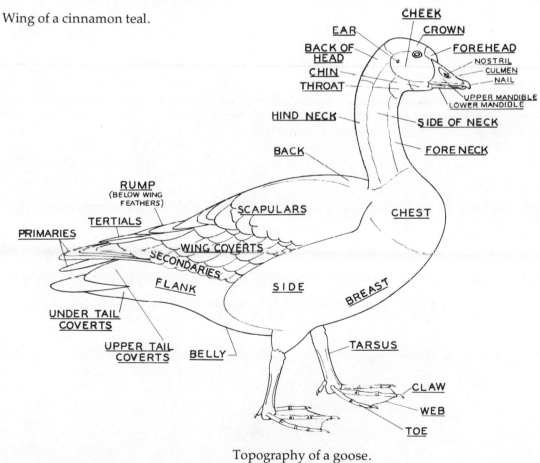

Topography of a goose.

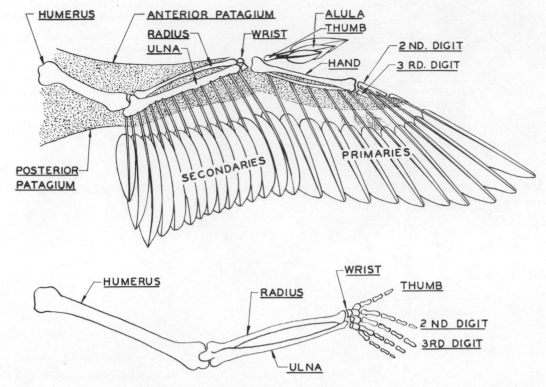

Comparison of a duck's wing with a man's arm.

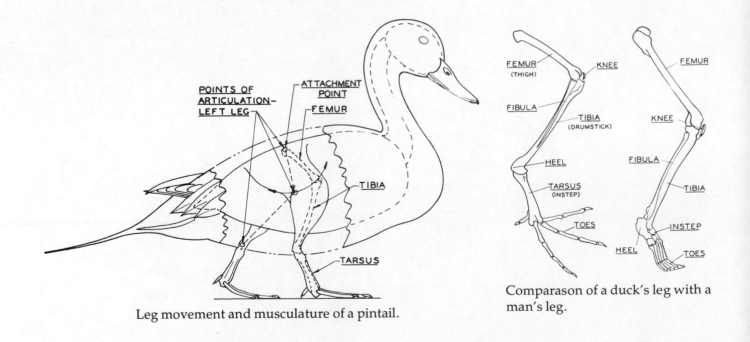

Leg movement and musculature of a pintail.

Comparason of a duck's leg with a man's leg.

254